I0152919

A Hope-Filled Life

A Hope-Filled Life

The Significance of Hope in the Life of a Believer

JAMES R. WILKES

RESOURCE *Publications* • Eugene, Oregon

A HOPE-FILLED LIFE
The Significance of Hope in the Life of a Believer

Copyright © 2021 James R. Wilkes. All rights reserved. Except for brief quotations in critical publications or reviews, no part of this book may be reproduced in any manner without prior written permission from the publisher. Write: Permissions, Wipf and Stock Publishers, 199 W. 8th Ave., Suite 3, Eugene, OR 97401.

Unless otherwise indicated, Scripture quotations are from the ESV® Bible (The Holy Bible, English Standard Version®), copyright © 2001 by Crossway, a publishing ministry of Good News Publishers. Used by permission. All rights reserved.

Scripture quotations marked (NAS) are taken from the New American Standard Bible®,
Copyright © 1960, 1962, 1963, 1968, 1971, 1972, 1973, 1975, 1977, 1995 by The Lockman Foundation Used by permission. www.Lockman.org

Scripture quotations marked (NIV) are taken from the Holy Bible, New International Version®, NIV®. Copyright © 1973, 1978, 1984, 2011 by Biblica, Inc.™ Used by permission of Zondervan. All rights reserved worldwide. www.zondervan.com

The "NIV" and "New International Version" are trademarks registered in the United States Patent and Trademark Office by Biblica, Inc.™

Scripture quotations marked (NKJV) are taken from the New King James Version®. Copyright © 1982 by Thomas Nelson. Used by permission. All rights reserved.

Scriptures marked KJV are taken from the King James Version (KJV): King James Version, public domain.

Resource Publications
An Imprint of Wipf and Stock Publishers
199 W. 8th Ave., Suite 3
Eugene, OR 97401

www.wipfandstock.com

PAPERBACK ISBN: 978-1-7252-9281-9
HARDCOVER ISBN: 978-1-7252-9282-6
EBOOK ISBN: 978-1-7252-9283-3

02/09/21

Dedicated to the faithful saints at Grace Community Chapel
who truly were a great blessing to walk with in Christ

Contents

Preface

Hope is certainly a word that evangelical Christians are familiar with. At the same time, in my experience, it does not find itself center-stage in terms of its importance in the Christian life. Yet, it is a vital part of God's saving work in the lives of his children in any culture and at any time. I did a series of teaching lessons on Biblical hope a few years ago during our church's Wednesday evening Bible study. I chose that subject because I felt strongly that the believers I shepherded would benefit from some biblical and practical teaching on hope. I write this book because I believe that the subject is extremely important for all believers to understand. In the midst of much of our current evangelical culture, which has a tendency to sometimes emphasize only what is easy and simple to digest, can center on the self, and be pragmatically oriented, the importance of something like biblical hope can be overlooked. Christians need to understand biblical hope and its importance to our daily walk in Christ. Hope, for the Christian, is an everyday staple for a walk of faith.

This study is not exhaustive. I do not believe I have written everything that can be said of the hope that is revealed in Scripture. The goal for the book is to show how the hope we have in Christ is a significant aspect of one's Christian life. Biblical hope is not simply an abstraction, but a real grace given us by the Spirit of God. We walk by faith not sight, and we hope for that which we do not see. Faith and hope are both extremely important gifts given us by our gracious God. Our hope, though focused on the future promises of God, is a present reality. I cannot emphasize this enough. Hope may look forward, but is meant to be a present and significant encouragement, We must not lose hope in our walk in this present evil age, rather, we must be filled with hope. Biblical hope ought to continually be a major driving force in our faith journey.

It is my desire in these pages to express some substantial truths about how hope impacts one's Christian life. I seek to be biblical and desire to write in an easily comprehensible manner. It is my prayer that all genuine believers, no matter what level of maturity at the time of the reading of this book, will benefit spiritually from it. Even as we find our outer selves perishing, our heart is being renewed and strengthened everyday with hope. We must not lose heart. The race set before us has an end, and it is a glorious one. In the meantime, we must understand that all of God's promises have been secured for us by Jesus Christ himself.

Is this thing the Bible calls *hope* important? There should be no doubt in any Christian's mind concerning the answer to this question. It is an absolute essential of the Christian life. Hope is a gospel grace that brings forth joy in the Lord and endurance in life. That is why Peter, in the first imperative (command) of his first epistle calls us to "set your hope fully on the grace that will be brought to you at the revelation of Jesus Christ" (1 Peter 1:13). May the Lord use his truths concerning hope to enable you to adhere to this command.

1

God: The Center of Our Hope

Hope is a pretty popular word in the English language. It is commonly used to express anticipation of something that one desires to happen but may or may not happen. The outcome is not certain but one *hopes* for it. One may hope that it doesn't rain on a certain day because of an upcoming outdoor event. We hope that our favorite team wins the upcoming big game. Sometimes our hopes are simply wishful thinking. We hope for things that are unlikely to ever happen. The word is sometimes used in conjunction with the word *dream*. We might say to someone, "May all your hopes and dreams come true." In today's culture, the idea is for young people to "dream big!" This means that young people should seek to attain things that might seem too far out of reach for them. They should still strive for these things however, for hopes and dreams can come true.

Well, this book is about hope, but with a completely different meaning than any kind of wishful thinking. In this book, the concern is for the way the Scriptures use the word *hope*. I am seeking to express what might be called a "theology of hope." The reason for this is because hope is one of the most important parts of the Christian life. God desires that his children live hope-filled lives, and this book is seeking to flesh out what that means. So this book is written especially for those who follow Jesus Christ. It is for those that God has saved by grace through faith. It is for those who have embraced by faith the saving gospel. This book is about how we who belong to Jesus are very different from the world (those who are still in unbelief). One of the most significant differences between believers and unbelievers can be described as real, genuine, gospel-centered, Christ-exalting hope!

Hope is probably a familiar word to you if you are a Christian. You cannot help but notice it when you read your Bible. It's everywhere! The word itself appears some 151 times in the English Standard Version of the Bible. Not only do we read about it in Scripture, but we also sing so many hymns and praise songs that include the word *hope*. However, as popular a Christian word as *hope* is, I suspect that we might use it a lot and not actually grasp its full and rich meaning. Further, I suspect that quite often we think and behave in less than biblically hopeful ways in spite of our constant use of the word. I know personally that I need to grow in this area of hope. As believers, we normally hear a lot concerning Christian *faith*, and a lot concerning Christian *love*, but perhaps not so much about *hope*. So, this is a book that focusses on Christian hope. That makes it also a book about God, for our God is the God of hope (Romans 15:13), and it is on this God that our hope is set (1 Timothy 4:10). God and hope go together for the believer in Christ. This book is all about how they go together.

God Does Not Want to Fulfill All Your Hopes and Dreams

The hope we want to discuss in this book is extraordinary and life changing. What we want to get clear right from the start is that the gospel is not for fixing up all your temporal problems and removing the obstacles for your self-appointed successes. If you know Christ, then be sure that your salvation involves something far better than whatever your hopes and dreams were before you came to Christ. It may well be that some of the hopes and dreams of your old self still linger. You must understand you have been brought into a whole new realm of existence. Paul puts it this way in Colossians 1:13, "He has delivered us from the domain of darkness and transferred us to the kingdom of his beloved Son." We have experienced a realm shift! *Realm* is a domain or area ruled by something. For example, my wife might say to me "stay out of my kitchen" when she is cooking and feels my presence would be a hindrance. She is, in essence, saying to me that the kitchen is her realm. Well, we have been brought into Jesus' realm! The implications are huge for our lives now and for our future. In salvation, God has already moved us into the realm of Christ's kingdom. Christ's kingdom is not all about the hopes and dreams of finite and fallen human beings. God does not want to fulfill all of your hopes and dreams. God does not want all of your trials and troubles to magically disappear so that you can be happy, healthy, and move up the ladder of success to what you imagine are greener pastures. The good news is that Christian hope is much deeper, far richer, and considerably superior to these kinds of temporal wishes. The gospel of Jesus Christ deals in ultimate things. It goes beyond this life, yet, it deals with the real needs we have in this life. The gospel saves us from our narcissism and yet brings us something more glorious than us, something eternally satisfying! We don't always see our real needs clearly. Sin blocks our spiritual vision at times. We need to understand our real problems and embrace God's all-satisfying answer. This is what biblical hope is all about. It is hope brought to our hearts by the Spirit of God through the cross of Jesus Christ as ordained by God the Father. This hope is a reality because the God of hope has moved in our hearts by grace, and we have believed in the hope that the gospel brings. His revealed truth and his exceedingly great promises have been embraced. This is hope because God is seen as the prize the believer in Christ is running the race to obtain. This is not a hope for self-glory. It is not a hope guided by the self-absorbed tendencies of the culture of this present evil age. It is not a hope secured by one's own performance. It comes to a person based on Christ's merits not one's own. It comes solely by the grace of God. It is secured by the work of Christ. It is received by faith. Thus, it is a hope that belongs to the Christian alone and God is at the very center of it.

Knowing God

If you have embraced the gospel, you have undoubtedly recognized you are a sinner by nature and by activity. In other words, sin comes from a sinful heart and works its way out into sinful thoughts, words, and deeds. You have trusted Christ to save you recognizing his redeeming work on the cross and his resurrection signifying the victory of the cross. Thus, you have been saved from the wrath of God. Hopefully, you have also realized that redemption involves being saved *from* something *to* something. God saves us from sin. God saves us to himself. This is what eternal life is all about. It is about knowing and enjoying God forever. Knowing God is a great, great thing. There is, of course, one greater thing than knowing God. As J. I. Packer says in his classic work *Knowing God*, "What matters supremely, therefore, is not, in the last analysis, the fact that I know God, but the larger fact that underlies it—the fact that *he knows me*."[1] God knew us in a saving way before the world began and set his affection on us. We know him because he first knew us! Consequently, Christ purchased eternal life for us. Titus 1:2 reads, "In hope of eternal life, which God, who never lies, promised before the ages began." In knowing Christ, we have eternal life now, but we do not have it in its fullness. So Paul, in Titus 1:2, speaks of our being in hope of eternal life. This is the hope of every believer. Although there is a sense in which we possess eternal life beginning at conversion, here we think of it in terms of the fullness which is yet to come. Eternal life is not simply about quantity. It is about knowing God. Listen to Christ's prayer in John 17:1–3.

> "When Jesus had spoken these words, he lifted up his eyes to heaven, and said, 'Father, the hour has come; glorify your Son that the Son may glorify you, since you have given him authority over all flesh, to give eternal life to all whom you have given him. And this is eternal life, that they know you the only true God, and Jesus Christ whom you have sent.'"

1. J. I. Packer, *Knowing God* (Illinois: InterVarsity Press, 1973), 41

Eternal life means knowing God and being fully satisfied in him. It means being brought into his presence to glorify him forever. For fallen sinful creatures, it requires God's grace in Jesus Christ for this to happen. Believers know a salvation that is by grace alone, through faith alone, in Christ alone, and for God's glory alone. Our tendency is to gravitate toward the temporal, seeing very narrowly in our own little world. Believers must see big-picture things and live in light of them. The gospel is not just a three or four step formula that is followed by a prayer and then you are done and it is time to move on to something else. When one embraces Christ by faith, one is transferred into the kingdom of Christ and is then exhorted to set one's mind on kingdom things. The believer is brought personally into God's redemptive story and looks forward joyfully to the blessed hope and glorious appearing of Christ. We must not think of Christian hope in terms of fleshly and worldly satisfactions. We look for Christ to come and his kingdom to come in its fullness so that we may be in his presence forever. This is our hope. This comes to us from God. This hope is central to our lives. It drives us. Or at least, it should! It might help here to think a few moments about life as fallen and finite human beings apart from knowing God. Let's look at some important truths about humanity we should know.

Knowing Our Fallen Humanity

Human life is completely dependent on God. God is self-existing and independent. He has life in himself. In fact, God is completely happy in himself (in the persons of the Trinity—Father, Son, and Holy Spirit). He created humanity out of his love and his desire to share himself. He created us to enjoy him. So human life is created. It comes from God's life and is completely dependent upon him (Acts 17:24,25). Therefore God expects us to be thankful for our lives. Please let this sink in. Because we are alive and our being alive is from God, he expects us to be grateful for the life he has given us. It should be natural to be glad to be living, glad to exist. God expects us to honor him as the one who gives us our very existence. We should acknowledge that it is good to be alive and thus, God is to be thanked and praised (Romans 1:21). It is normal for us to want to be alive. It is normal for human beings to enjoy the gifts of living that God, in his common grace, gives even to fallen and sinful creatures. The idea here is that we should appreciate the fact that we exist. I am alive! If you are reading this, then so are you! This life comes from God. He is to be praised and thanked. This is how it should be, but it is not how it is in our fallen and finite world. Chapter One of the book of Romans makes it very clear that fallen human beings, instead of honoring and thanking the living and true God for life, seek out that which is not God and glorify what is created rather than glorify the living and true God (Romans 1:21–23).

So, human beings presume that it is their right to be alive. They act as if they were alive independently of God. The truth is our every breath comes from him, and apart from his sustaining us we would not be in existence. This is a root sin. We are guilty of presuming we have a right to exist and deserve life. The fact that we are fallen sinners makes this all the more wicked. But the truth is that we are fallen creatures. It should be clear there is something radically wrong with the world. It has been cursed by God and is filled with fallen sinners. Human beings come into this world separated from God. Thus, we are not only not thankful for life, but we are rebellious in that we do not worship God or love others as we should. We enter the world under the just wrath and condemnation of God (Romans 1:18). So what is missing is life with God! And this is where the gospel comes into play. Christ brings us new life! He takes undeserving rebels and gives them a new heart. He reconciles sinners to God by absorbing God's wrath for sin on the cross. When sinners embrace the gospel, wrath is removed and sin is covered. There is reconciliation with God. We are new in Christ. Second Corinthians 5:17 says, "Therefore, if anyone is in Christ, he is a new creation. The old has passed away; behold, the new has come." There is no more condemnation. All this happens by the grace of God. And now, for that very important part: this new life is life with God. It is life that is awaiting its fullness to come. That is our hope. That is the essence of Christian hope—life with God in its fullness. Do you see your life as a life filled with hope in God? Because of the gospel, is it now really good to be alive? As a believer, even in facing the final enemy, death, there is great hope in Christ. Paul makes an amazing statement in Philippians 1:21. He says, "to die is gain"! He goes on to explain in v.23 that this is so because it means "to depart and be with Christ." Life with God—that is the essence of hope.

Life with God as Our Ultimate Hope

Some years ago, late one night, I drove from Boston to my home, about a forty-minute drive south of Boston. When I got home, I was alone in my small house. I laid face down on my living room floor and cried out to God for most of the rest of the night. I was fifty-two years old. You see, when I left Boston, I left my wife in a hospital bed awaiting surgery. The next morning she would have coronary artery by-pass surgery. It was not what we were expecting or had planned. We were told by the medical staff that the surgery needed to be done right away because of the blockage in her arteries. I cried out to God, "O God, please don't take my wife from me." I cried out over and over again. It was with great anguish of soul. In moments like these, prayer flows from one's lips without having to do much deep thinking. The next morning, my wife had her surgery. It went well. Her recovery went well. God answered prayer. Many years have gone by since then, and she is doing very well. I praise God for his mercy and grace given to us during that time! How gracious is our God! But more importantly, I praise God for the hope my wife and I both had then that did not depend on the outcome of the surgery. Please do not misunderstand. I am very thankful that it was part of his good purposes not to take my wife at that time. Mary and I feel so blessed to be spending this part of our lives together. But our hope is not that we will someday retire and live out a cozy, comfy life with one another. Our hope is not that all of our physical afflictions will be healed in this life. Our hope is not even that when we die we will go to a better place (although as believers, upon death our souls will go to be with Christ—and that certainly is a better place.). Our hope (the ultimate hope the Bible points us to) is that Jesus will come again and fix the brokenness we now experience because of the fall of man into sin. There will be the resurrection of the body, the renewal of this world into an eternal paradise, and life everlasting as God dwells with his people (Revelation 21:3)! Our hope is that we will glorify and enjoy God forever in everlasting blessedness. Again, we have this hope by grace alone, in Christ alone, and through faith alone. We look forward to forever making much of God! We recognize that making much of God is not simply the result of our joy in him, but it is the culmination of the joy itself! In other words, we will enjoy making much of God. To some this may sound crazy, but this is at the heart of Christian hope—life with God! He is truly at the very center of biblical hope.

2

Hope Defined

As I mentioned in the first chapter, there is a lot of teaching on faith and love being done today in evangelical Christianity. This is, of course, a good thing. But we must not underestimate the important part Christian hope plays in our walk with Jesus Christ. Does hope play a significant role in your Christian life? When is the last time you thought about hope and what it means? In a culture filled with anxiety, depression, and gloom, Christian hope brings glory to God as it lifts the soul away from despair and into delight in God. In this book, I might refer to it as Christian hope, biblical hope, or gospel hope. I mean the very same thing. I mean the hope we have in Jesus Christ alone. I mean the hope we have because of his person and work.

Truly, our hope is in Christ alone. We sing hymns about this hope constantly in our churches. But we must do more than sing the words however wonderful they are. We must understand the truths from Scripture that undergird the words. We must grow in our knowledge and understanding of gospel truth in order for our hope to be powerful and life-transforming and enduring. In *New Morning Mercies*, Paul David Tripp states, "If your hope disappoints you, it's because it is the wrong hope." He goes on to say "hope that simply will never ever disappoint us—can only be found in one place. It is not to be found in a certain thing, it is, in fact, a person,

Jesus."[1] In this chapter, I want to look into the Word of God and add some substantial propositional truth to what it means to say that Christ alone is our hope. Here is a good working definition: Hope is a gospel grace that brings forth joy in the Lord and endurance in life, as one rests confidently in God's faithful fulfillment of future promises. It is a *grace*, which means it is an undeserved gift given to those who are ill-deserving (deserving of condemnation and God's eternal wrath). It is a *gospel grace*, which means it comes through the work of Jesus Christ on our behalf. It is about God's *faithful fulfillment of promises*, which means God will do for us what he has said he would. Let's explore now more deeply just what we should mean as believers in Christ when we use the word hope. Here are six statements that taken together give us a fairly thorough definition of biblical hope.

Biblical Hope Is the Joyful and Confident Expectation for Those in Christ of All the Future Fulfillment of Redemptive Promises that will be Consummated at His Coming

First Peter 1:13 states, "Therefore, preparing your minds for action, and being sober-minded, set your hope fully on the grace that will be brought to you at the revelation of Jesus Christ." In this verse, we have the first clear command verb in Peter's letter, "set your hope." We find in 1 Peter what we find in many places in the New Testament. God's commands follow explanations of what God has done and is doing. In the first twelve verses of 1 Peter, we have many wonderful truths about what the Lord has done for us and is doing for us in the gospel (these statements of truth could be called indicatives—statements of fact). Only after speaking to his readers about these wonderful things, does Peter now give commands (or imperatives). This pattern is known as the indicatives before the imperatives. The point is that believers need to act on the basis of what God has and is doing on their behalf. We must understand our actions flow from God's working! We move in the Christian life

---

1. Paul David Tripp, *New Morning Mercies: A Daily Gospel Devotional* (Illinois: Crossway, 2014), January 23 reading

on the basis of God's enabling grace in the gospel. Here we can set our hope fully on the grace to be brought to us because Peter has already told us the wonderful truth that we have "been born again to a living hope through the resurrection of Jesus Christ from the dead" (1 Peter 1:3). Peter has also spoken of an inheritance reserved for us who are being kept by the power of God (1 Peter 1:4–5). This is why we can fully set our hope on future grace given to us at the return of Christ. Peter first gave us twelve verses of glorious gospel truths and then says in v.13, "therefore"—because of these truths—we can fully set our hope on the future graces to be received at Christ's coming. All of these things come to us because of Christ's redemptive sacrifice on the cross.

Someday Jesus Christ will return as promised. There will be a final judgment. Believers will be publicly proclaimed righteous (as has already happened ahead of time in our justification). What grace will be shown on that day to those who have trusted Jesus Christ! We can now await that day with joy and confidence because our salvation is all God's work by his grace. Hope means we are resting securely in Christ. When we embraced Christ through faith by grace, his righteousness was imputed to us. This means it was counted as if it were ours. Our sin was taken away by him. The work he achieved on the cross was applied to us. He even purchased grace for our very conversion! The initial faith at conversion continues. Genuine faith is a sustained posture not a temporary and superficial moment. The believer must continually look to him. We must never think we can relate to God based on our own merit. Our relationship with God is always because of Christ's cross. Thus, we expect, with eyes of faith, to see all of his promises come to pass. Some promises are for every day. Some are especially necessary to grab hold of during difficult times of affliction. But he continues to be faithful. So we set our hope in him because of his grace culminating in the great grace we will know at Christ's second coming. Hope is joyful confidence. What joy it is to know that when he comes (or when we die), we will be welcomed not condemned. What joy it is to know that we will enter his kingdom in its fullness when he returns. Let me interject here that the ultimate hope of the believer as seen in Scripture is not what happens to us at death.

While it is true that at death the believer's soul is present with the Lord, it is bodily resurrection that is the believer's final destiny. We could say resurrection is our ultimate eschatological (meaning *future*) hope. When Christ brings in the fullness of his kingdom at his second coming, our hope will be realized. Even now, in the midst of spiritual warfare, and the serious "fight of faith" that must take place in accordance with it, Peter tells us to set our hope on the grace of God!

Although Biblical Hope Is About Future Promises, It Is Experienced in the Present as We Anticipate, with Patience, Future Blessedness—Meaning Perfect Joy in God

Please notice Peter encourages believers in the above verse (1 Peter 1:13) to have this hope in future grace right now. Hope is for now. It is to be a present reality. Not only is God's faithfulness real but our hope in that which is presently unseen is also to be real. In fact, since God is the God of hope, Paul tells us our hope should abound because we have the Spirit of God. "May the God of hope fill you with all joy and peace in believing, so that by the power of the Holy Spirit you may abound in hope" (Romans 15:13). The present indwelling of God's Spirit is the source and security of our hope. So hope is experienced right now. In the midst of spiritual battles, our hope spurs us on. With trials and afflictions in our lives, we look to our faithful God and his promise of the fullness of eternal life. God has already saved us (past), is currently saving us (present), and will completely save us (future). The good news safeguards our hope right now. We must look outside of ourselves to the God who is working continually to bring us safely home. Our hope is not in our performance before God for, if such were the case, we would fail. The gospel is not God giving us a second chance. God could give us a million chances. We are sinners. We would not succeed in earning his favor or his future blessings. The gospel is a rescue mission successfully performed by Christ. This is why we experience hope in the present. Our hope is in him!

Biblical Hope Is Not Exclusively about Final Redemption but Also about Confidently Expecting God to be Faithful in All of What Has Not Yet Transpired in Our Lives

Although biblical hope points to the ultimate promises involved in Christ's coming, we also confidently expect God to be faithful in all of his promises that have an ongoing nature. This aspect of hope goes like this: I do not know what my tomorrows in this present evil age will be, but I know that they are in God's sovereign hands, and this is the God who has told me that he is for me and will never leave me and that his grace is sufficient! You see, our hope is in God's steadfast love and in God's word to us. Psalm 147:11 tell us "the LORD takes pleasure in those who fear him, in those who hope in his steadfast love." So if I see an impending trial, my heart can be filled with hope knowing that through that trial God does not stop loving me. He does not stop being merciful and gracious to me. He is still my heavenly Father. Jesus will not leave or forsake me. In Psalm 119:114 the psalmist proclaims, "You are my hiding place and my shield; I hope in your word." God's word maps out for us the workings of his steadfast love! So every day my hope can be in the truth that his mercies are new every morning—great is his faithfulness (Lamentations 3:22–23). When discouraged about situations that are not working out as I had thought they would, I can take comfort in the truths of Romans 8:28–39: God is working in my life for ultimate good, he is for me therefore nothing or no one can ultimately be against me, he does not condemn me, and nothing can separate me from his love! I do not know how situations in my life will turn out, but I know that his word is truth and his steadfast love and faithfulness are real. So I can confidently *expect God to be faithful* (read this *hope*) even as life's events unfold some very difficult situations. As believers, we must know this is not our best life now. We have this wonderfully glorious eschatological hope. Nonetheless, even as we live out this life, we can expect God to be graciously working. I am simply saying here that our hope extends to the unknowns of this life as well as the blessed hope of the life to come!

Faith and Hope Are Inextricably Linked Together: Without Faith, There Is No Hope; and with Genuine Faith, There is Genuine Hope

Hebrews 11:1 states, "Now faith is the assurance of things hoped for, the conviction of things not seen." Hope is the extension of faith into the future. The future promises of God are all real. They all will operate in their own time. We wait for them to come to pass. Our faith assures us they will. Consider Paul's words in Romans 8:24–25: "Now hope that is seen is not hope. For who hopes for what he sees? But if we hope for what we do not see, we wait for it with patience." The important thing to note here is that we wait with patience for that which we hope for. One of the things that Paul is referring to in Romans 8 is "the redemption of our bodies" (Romans 8:23). Paul explains that we are waiting for the glorified body promised us when Christ returns (Philippians 3:20–21). This is when suffering will be done away with. This is when death will be no more. This is when sin will be forever put out of Christ's kingdom. Most importantly, this is when we will be in the presence of God forever! We believe this because God has promised it (Revelation 21:3–4). We wait because it has certainly not happened yet. We hope because we do believe it will happen. Do you see how faith and hope are linked together? So it is extremely important to know what the future promises of God really are (and we will explore this further along). It is important also to personally embrace these promises. Our hope is always based firmly on what God has revealed to us in his Word. Our hope is always that which Jesus has secured for us in his redemptive work. His resurrection has secured ours!

Let us consider for a moment the truth of 1 Corinthians 15:20, "But in fact Christ has been raised from the dead, the firstfruits of those who have fallen asleep." This verse teaches us that Christ's resurrection is decisive for the resurrection of all believers. Christ's resurrection is why I can look forward to my own resurrection. Christ's resurrection is a pledge of the resurrections of all who are in Christ—because he lives, we will live. Paul declares in 1 Corinthians 15 that the resurrection of Christ is inextricably linked with the resurrection of believers. Because one happens (Christ's resurrection) then the other must certainly happen as well (all in Christ). Christ is the *firstfruits*. The concept of firstfruits referred to the idea that a first portion of the harvest was set aside for an offering to God before the rest of the harvest could be used for other things. The firstfruits thus consecrated the whole harvest. Christ was the first of the resurrected in glorious bodies, bodies that would die no more. All those to be resurrected follow Christ's resurrection. Firstfruits necessarily implies more fruits to come. Christ is the firstfruits of the harvest; the rest of the harvest has been put on hold, so to speak so that there can be a much greater reaping. We have not seen our resurrection bodies. Our faith in Christ's resurrection extends into hope of our future resurrection. You see, I think, how faith and hope are inextricably linked together.

Hope Is the Confidence That It Really Is Going to Turn Out Alright; It Is Not an Unfounded Optimism but a Powerful Conviction That Drives Out Despair

The first statement about hope in this chapter used the words *confident expectation*. In this part of our definition note the word *confidence*. Biblical hope is not a maybe or could be. It is not wishful thinking. It is based on what God has declared to be so. It makes no difference that God has declared it to be so for the future. God brings to pass all that he purposes to bring to pass. He is God! Psalm 33:11 encourages us in this certainty: "The counsel of the LORD stands forever, the plans of his heart to all generations." Consider also Ephesians 1:11: "In him we have obtained an inheritance, having been predestined according to the purpose of him who works all things according to the counsel of his will." The gospel is not an instant "fix-it" gospel in which God quickly solves all of your temporal problems and grants all of your dreams to come true. However, in the absolute sense, everything does turn out alright in the end (*alright* here being a giant understatement). By this I mean that the believer will have fullness of joy in the presence of God forever (Psalm 16:11). This hope is not an unfounded optimism. It rests in the steadfast love and faithfulness of the living and true God.

Unfortunately many believers do look at the gospel in the wrong way. The gospel is seen as that which will solve their marriage problems or financial difficulties or get them their dream job. The gospel does not promise any of these things. It is not magic. It is not one's good luck charm. Although, when one has a new heart in Christ, these things could surely turn around, that is not what the gospel promises. It promises something far deeper and more significant. The gospel is for forgiveness of sin and reconciliation with God. It is about the fulfillment of the purpose man was originally created for. It is about rescue from God's eternal wrath. It is about satisfaction in the only one who can truly satisfy. It is about being brought into the love of the Triune God forever. These are the things that drive out despair. These are the things that get us through the darkest times. Our temporal troubles cannot compare with the eternal glory of knowing God. Paul calls these temporal troubles "slight momentary affliction" in 2 Corinthians 4:17! This is not to minimize any affliction or sorrow you might be going through. There is certainly great suffering in this fallen world. Some trials are enormous burdens to be borne. Paul's point is that when compared to the weight of glory in God's eternal kingdom, to say "it will be worth it all" doesn't really fully express the glories of God's kingdom to come!

The Christian's Hope Is Rooted in the Person and Work of Jesus Christ; In Other Words, Our Hope Is Grounded in the Gospel and Dependent Fully on God

I cannot emphasize enough that our hope comes from outside of us. Listen to the psalmist: "Put not your trust in princes, in a son of man, in whom there is no salvation. When his breath departs he returns to the earth; on that very day his plans perish. Blessed is he whose help is the God of Jacob, whose hope is in the LORD his God" (Psalm 146:3–5). Mere human beings cannot bring us biblical hope. We don't earn this hope. We don't perform for this hope. Christ earned it. He lived the righteous life that we could not live. He died an atoning death in the place of sinners. his righteousness was imputed upon us and our sin was taken away by him. This is the good news. Our salvation comes from our Triune God. God the Father administered it as he sent his Son into the world. God the Son accomplished it as he lived in perfect righteousness and died in the sinner's place. Then he rose from the grave in victory. God the Spirit applied it as he made us who were dead in sin alive with faith as a result of the new birth. The Spirit brings Christ's life to us. Salvation is of the Lord! Hope is of the Lord, as well!

It is so important to constantly be aware that our hope lies in what God has done for us in the gospel. It is so important that we never think of our hope as being earned or achieved by ourselves. When unbelievers (those without hope) encounter believers, what should they see and hear? They should see joyful and hopeful people. But they should not be given the impression believers are joyful and hopeful in themselves. They should not be given the impression believers think themselves better than others. They should see neither self-righteousness nor despair. They should see joy in God. They should see humble dependency upon God. Unbelievers ought to hear from our lips humble gospel words, words pointing them to Christ alone. They should hear how great our God is. How marvelous are his wonderful works. Our testimony should not focus on ourselves but on the one who died for us and rose again. Our salvation testimony ought to be about the great forgiveness of sin granted to undeserving sinners through Jesus Christ. It should then move on to the most amazing and wonderful point. This salvation brings us into a relationship of joy in God. It is not simply a way to have a better life now. It is about knowing the living and true God who created us to be satisfied in him alone. Hope-filled hearts should have their roots in the gospel of Jesus Christ.

3

Reasons Hope Is Important

So far, we have seen that life with God is the ultimate object of our hope. We have looked at six statements that give us an overall picture of what we are talking about when we speak of biblical hope. In this chapter we want to examine why hope is so important for living the Christian life. We want to explore ways that hope makes a difference in the way we live. Does it make a difference? When it comes to living day by day, are Christians pretty much the same as everyone else except for the fact that they go to heaven when they die? If our lives truly are different than the lives of unbelievers, how does hope play a part in it? The goal of this chapter is to elaborate on the answers to these questions. The concise answers are: yes, hope makes a huge difference; and, no, Christians live completely different lives than unbelievers. Before looking at some important points, allow me to give a personal illustration that demonstrates the way hope can be used by God to change lives.

When my wife and I were married almost five years, we moved to a part of Massachusetts that we were not very familiar with. Though we had lived in the state all of our lives, we moved south of Boston after living in the northern suburbs of Boston previously. My wife was a little lonely for we were far enough away from our friends and family that we did not see them as often, especially during the work week. So when a woman (let's call her

Jane) came to our house selling cosmetics one day, my wife (let's call her *Mary*; actually that is her name!) was, perhaps, a little more eager than most people to speak to this door-to-door sales person. Mary was friendly enough to Jane that she made return trips to the house to show her new products and try to make a sale. We were on a tight budget at the time, so Mary had not bought any items. Nonetheless, Jane kept coming back and the two ladies were having friendly conversations. Jane even shared some things with Mary about her personal life. She had experienced some pretty difficult circumstances, but, nonetheless, as she related them to Mary, she never complained or spoke badly of the people causing her these hardships. Her attitude and demeanor did not seem consistent with her difficult circumstances. In fact, Jane appeared to be joyful with no signs of despair or hopelessness. After several visits, while they were chatting away one day, Mary asked Jane if she could ask a personal question. The question she asked was this: "Why are you so joyful?" Jane replied, "Do you really want to know!" Then she proceeded to tell her that it was because of her relationship with Jesus Christ. That was the day my wife embraced the gospel! Yes, biblical hope makes a difference in one's earthly walk. This woman's hope, a hope that filled her heart, came through in her life. It made a significant difference, and as a result, it made an eternal difference in my wife's life (and mine as well, for I was not a believer at the time). Let me share with you four ways that the kind of hope we have been talking about meaningfully affects our lives.

Biblical Hope Produces Joy

In the middle of a number of exhortations in Romans 12, Paul states in verse 12, "Rejoice in hope." Of course, Romans 12 follows Paul's remarkable explanation of the gospel of Jesus Christ in chapters 1–11. It is only out of the gospel's grace that our progressive sanctification (spiritual growth) flows. Spiritual growth flows out from the gospel and our union with Christ. A significant part of this particular truth is that joy flows out from hope. Hope flows out of the gospel. We look forward with confidence in the Lord to all that he has promised to do! Out of this kind of hope comes our great joy. Joy is inseparably linked to the Christian life. All of it! We are not supposed to pick and choose when joy is appropriate or not appropriate. We may have many other feelings along with joy, but we are not supposed to be joyless at any time. Martin Luther states this about joy: "God loveth not heaviness and doubtfulness of spirit: he hateth unsound doctrines, and sorrowful cogitations; and he loveth cheerful hearts."[1] The Scriptures tell us to "Rejoice in the Lord always" (Philippians 4:4). Joy is the great gladness of heart that results as we know and treasure God properly. It grows as we know and treasure God more and more. A lack of joy shows a lack of satisfaction in God (Matthew 13:44; Psalm 90:14). As members of the new realm of Christ's kingdom, joy is to be a distinguishing mark of our lives. Romans 14:17 tells us that the kingdom of God is characterized by "righteousness, peace, and joy in the Holy Spirit." God doesn't change. Our God is good, gracious, and glorious. Because he has set his steadfast love upon every believer in Christ, we can always rejoice in him. This confident expectation we have in Christ and his precious promises causes us to be filled with joy right now. Remember, although hope's expectations are future, hope is a present experience, a right-now experience. The Spirit of God causes us to abound in hope and this same Spirit fills us with joy as well. Here is how Paul put it in Romans 15:13, "May the God of hope fill you with all joy and peace in believing, so that by the power of the Holy Spirit you may abound in hope."

Please understand that I am not saying that the Christian life is always easy. It is not. We endure hardness as good soldiers in Christ. There will be opposition and there will be suffering. Also, please do not get the idea that because the believer is to always have joy that we must think of all of our circumstances as good. Some are not good. Bad things do happen. The believer is not supposed to call what is bad, good. The believer is to recognize that even the bad is used by God to accomplish his good purposes. There are no accidents. There are no mistakes made by God. Each thing is brought into our lives through his sovereign will. God works in it

1. Martin Luther, Commentary on Galatians (Michigan, Kregel Classics, 1979), 350

all for good. That is the promise of Romans 8:28: "And we know that for those who love God all things work together for good, for those who are called according to his purpose." God has his purposes even in the bad things that come into our lives. We must not be disappointed in God's sovereignly directed purposes. Instead, in the midst of our pain and affliction, in the midst even of our sorrow, our hope in God brings joy. Not only is a heart that has both joy and sorrow not a contradiction, it is to be expected (John 16:33).

Biblical Hope Produces Endurance

One of the most neglected doctrines of the Scriptures, I think, is the doctrine of the believer's perseverance. It is beyond the scope of this writing to develop this doctrine.[2] For our purposes, let us simply say that God calls his living saints to keep the faith to the end (Mark 13:13). he calls believers to run with endurance the race that is set before them (Hebrews 12:1). Not only does he call us to endure, but he assures us that we will endure for he gives us the effectual grace (*effectual* here means not simply an offer of grace but a dynamic grace that accomplishes what God wills) to persevere. Our salvation is secure but, nonetheless, we must persevere (Colossians 1:22–23).

One of the means for enduring hardness as good soldiers is our hope. Romans 8:25 states, "But if we hope for what we do not see, we wait for it with patience." The word *patience* here speaks of endurance. It means bearing up under difficult circumstances. It does not indicate a self-determining stamina. It indicates a bearing up because we are awaiting with confidence the culmination of God's redemptive work. We are waiting for Christ himself to bring in the fullness of his kingdom! With our eyes on the prize, so to speak, we persevere. The ultimate prize is God himself! He is our exceedingly great reward. I do not mean that we earn this reward. Jesus Christ has earned it. We receive it in him.

---

2. For a concise yet excellent work on perseverance, I recommend Thomas R. Schreiner, *Run to Win the Prize* (Illinois: Crossway, 2010); for a longer more thorough work see Thomas R. Schreiner, Ardel B. Caneday, *The Race Set Before Us* (Illinois: InterVarsity Press, 2001)

Believers must face the difficult realities of life head on with hope. Again, this means trusting God to fulfill all of his promises, including the truth that his grace is sufficient (2 Corinthians 12:9). Paul speaks of the steadfastness of our hope in 1 Thessalonians 1:3. The expression means that the believer's steadfastness is produced by hope. Hope drives us. In fact, although it can be said that our faith drives our hope, it can also be said that our hope energizes one's faith and love. That is what Paul says happened in the Colossian church. Paul writes, "since we heard of your faith in Christ Jesus and of the love that you have for all the saints, *because* (italics mine) of the hope laid up for you in heaven. Of this you have heard before in the word of the truth, the gospel" (Colossians 1:4–5).

Most believers have sung the great hymn of the faith "Amazing Grace." Many are aware that the words were written by John Newton who lived a really blasphemous life before conversion. Newton was involved in slave trading during his life (1725–1807), even captaining several slave ships. After conversion, Newton over time turned from his sinful lifestyle and spent the remainder of his life as an Anglican minister of the gospel, serving his congregations with great love. There is one stanza of Amazing Grace that perhaps you have never considered. I bring it up here because it speaks to the great doctrine of perseverance.

> Through many dangers, toils, and snares,
> I have already come;
> 'tis grace hath brought me safe thus far,
> and grace will lead me home.

Notice that our lives are filled with many "dangers, toils, and snares" according to Newton. Notice though how we are led safely home through all of them—by God's amazing grace! This is speaking of God's dynamic grace that enables us to persevere. Part of that grace is the enablement to look outside of ourselves to Christ. We look to the gospel. We look to the promises. We look to his strength that comes through his sufficient grace. It is common to hear a believer say that God will not give them more than they can handle, but this is not the biblical picture. God gives us many things that we cannot handle. We must rather think that God never gives us anything that he cannot handle! He sometimes overwhelms us with affliction so that we will look outside of ourselves to him. Paul spoke of his own affliction in this way: "For we do not want you to be ignorant, brothers, of the affliction we experienced in Asia. For we were so utterly burdened beyond our strength that we despaired of life itself. Indeed, we felt that we had received the sentence of death. But that was to make us rely not on ourselves but on God who raises the dead" (2 Corinthians 1:8–9). Thus, our hearts must be filled with confidence in him. Our hearts are filled with real hope. Hope is an endurance producer. God's grace will bring me home safely. God's grace will preserve me. Hope means waiting with endurance.

Biblical Hope Stabilizes the Soul

We live in a world where instability abounds. There is rapid change in culture. What is *in* yesterday is not *in* today. Today's *hot* items will run their course rather quickly and be replaced fairly soon. In my lifetime, I went from vinyl records to 8 track tapes to cassette tapes to cd's. But now, the trend is to stream music from the internet. However, I find it interesting that vinyl records and the turntables to play them on are making a comeback! As technology advances, I find that I cannot keep up with it all. Some changes, of course, are much more serious than others. I grew up during the cold war with the Soviet Union. There is no more Soviet Union. However, there are certainly threats to the world's safety among the nations of the world. I am exceedingly glad that our God is sovereign over them all (Psalm 33:10). I grew up watching black and white television. We had our choice of three stations! Now, I have cable TV and have my choice of over a hundred, but most of the programs on these stations are not worth watching. Yet again, things continue to change. Many people are abandoning cable TV and using channels that stream video for their television watching. In any event, I rather doubt anyone needs convincing that there are many instabilities in our present evil age. When thinking of instability we can also consider the ups and downs of life's circumstances. The economy goes up and down. The state of our health can sometimes go up and down.

Not much is certain. Our inner man (our soul) can get restless, discontent, and discouraged with all the change and uncertainty. There is, however, an answer to life's instability and vanity. The hope found in the gospel is the answer. It is our life-stabilizer. It brings certainty into this uncertain present evil age (If you notice that I use the expression "present evil age" a lot, it comes from Galatians 1:3). Hope in Christ brings stability to our unstable civilization.

The Scriptures call our gospel hope "the sure and steadfast anchor of the soul" (Hebrews 10:19). In the midst of life's uncertainties, we see God's future promises as realities that simply have not yet happened. We know that history is not simply a circular thing, always repeating itself. We know that history has a direction ordained by God. We know that he is in complete control. From creation, fall, redemption, and future consummation, God is directing the world toward his foreordained purposes for his glory. Thus, Jesus will return, the judgment of evil will take place, and he will make all things new (Revelation 21:5). I have heard the following illustration many times, but it really fits here so I will relate it, though I know not whether it really happened or not. Nonetheless, it makes a really good point. It seems that some seminary students found some free time and were playing basketball in a local gym. The janitor came in and they noticed that he sat down and was reading. They were curious. During a break in their game, they discovered that he was reading the Bible and, specifically, the book of Revelation. Deciding to have some fun, they began to quiz him a little. They asked if he understood what he was reading. Revelation is apocalyptic in its genre and symbol-laden, so they were surprised when the janitor replied that he did understand what he was reading. They seriously doubted it. When they asked him what the book of Revelation meant, his reply was concise but most profound. He said, "It means that Jesus wins!" That is it exactly. If you are a believer, do you understand that truth? Jesus wins. Through many dangers, toils, and snares, Jesus wins. Through great tribulation in the lives of the saints, Jesus wins. In the midst of an unstable world, Jesus wins. So, in spite of all the pessimism, in spite of all the negative news reporting, in spite of how things may appear, Jesus wins. In fact, he has been in control all along. In fact, he always wins! Our hope in him gives us this kind of stability in a crazy and unstable world.

Biblical Hope Purifies Us

When we say that biblical hope purifies us, we mean that it motivates us to grow in grace. It motivates us to be holy as our God is holy. It makes us desire to be like Christ in terms of his love and compassion. It makes us desire to be like Christ in terms of his desire to glorify his Father. We have the truth that biblical hope purifies us expressed in 1 John 3:2–3 which says, "Beloved, we are God's children now, and what we will be has not yet appeared; but we know that when he appears we shall be like him, because we shall see him as he is. And everyone who thus hopes in him purifies himself as he is pure." So, now we are God's children and what we will be has not yet appeared or been made known. This means that we cannot fully comprehend not only what life will be like in the eternal state but what *we* will be like in the eternal state. But we do know this: we shall be like Jesus because we shall see him as he is! The image of God we were originally created in will be restored fully and, further, unlike Adam and Eve, we will not have the potential to sin anymore. Upon seeing Christ at his appearing, there will be a transformation of whatever separates us from a full likeness at that time. Keep in mind this is not referring to what happens at a believer's death when the soul goes to be with Christ in what theologians call the intermediate state. This is referring to his second coming and the resurrection of the saints. Again, this is our great hope—this is what we are even now waiting for. It is what Paul referred to in Philippians 3:20,21, "But our citizenship is in heaven, and from it we await a Savior, the Lord Jesus Christ, who will transform our lowly body to be like his glorious body, by the power that enables him even to subject all things to himself." John is speaking in 1 John 3:2–3 of seeing Christ and being like him in a body like his glorified body. This is our final state and how we were created to be—body and soul and living in a paradise-temple (meaning in God's presence), worshipping and enjoying him and his abundant blessings forever.

Please understand, we will not become gods. We will be human beings in the fullest way possible in accordance with God's ultimate design and with the goal of glorifying God in this eternal state of being forever! This very hope motivates us. John is saying that those who have this hope, purify themselves as Christ is pure. This refers primarily to moral purity. It means we pursue holiness. We work at it as God works in us. John is saying here that if you have the hope of seeing Christ in his glory and being transformed into his likeness, this motivates you to be making progress even now. Second Corinthians 3:18 puts it this way: "And we all, with unveiled face, beholding the glory of the Lord, are being transformed into the same image from one degree of glory to another. For this comes from the Lord who is the Spirit." We see more and more of his glory through his revelation of himself in the Scriptures. We so admire him! We desire to be like him. Now, I do not mean that we desire to be God. Jesus is God and we will not nor can we be gods. We must not think like that. We are creatures made to reflect his glory not seek our own. We desire to reflect his glory by being like him in character. His Spirit is now indwelling us bringing forth fruit. The Spirit is producing the fruit of love which is reflected in the other fruit listed in Galatians 5:22–23. As we hope in him, this desire grows. We long for his coming. We long for his kingdom. We long to be completely freed from our sin that we may fully enjoy his presence. Is biblical hope an important part of our lives as believers of the gospel of Jesus Christ? Absolutely! For the above reasons and more, we need to see hope as a significant part of our Christian lives.

4

What Hope Is Not

One way to sharpen one's theological focus is to use negation. In seeking to understand truth, it helps to articulate what is not being said about a certain theological subject. In this chapter, we are going to do that with the matter of biblical hope. It is important for believers to recognize what biblical hope is not. Hope is an important reality of the Christian faith. Yet, as with any biblical truth, it can be misunderstood. So we want to present three statements of negation concerning our hope in Christ.

Hope in Christ Is Not Human Optimism

Hope is not simply another way of saying, "Hey, we need, as Christians, to have a positive outlook on life." I have known some Christians who attempt to offer comfort to other believers who are going through trials by saying things like, "You're going to get well, it is all going to be fine." That is human optimism not scriptural encouragement. If a believer is diagnosed with cancer, we can offer no certainty about the outcome of the treatment. We can however offer them the wonderful truth that for the believer, to die is to gain for it means departing to be with Christ (Philippians 1:21–23). If Christian parents have a rebellious teenager, we can offer no certainty in terms of the child's repentance. The Christian faith does not make us certain about all things. Our faith is about the redemptive narrative of Scripture and the doctrines that we derive from that narrative. The redemptive narrative involves creation, the fall, redemption, and the consummation of all things. In addition to the actual narrative passages that tell the Bible story, there are also what are called didactic (teaching) passages that teach the theology that undergirds the story. These didactic passages also bring the believer into the story. When Paul writes in Colossians 3:3, "For *you* have died, and *your* life is hidden with Christ in God" (italics mine)—I find myself in the redemptive story! I recognize that, as a believer, the *you* Paul is addressing includes me! I can confidently say that I, in some real sense, have died (the *old* me who was crucified with Christ is gone), and I can also say that I nevertheless live, hidden with Christ in God (I have been raised with him in new life, a life hidden with Christ in God). I am trying to make the point that I can be certain of these things because they are in God's Word which is truth. But there are many things that I simply do not know about. God's sovereign will in terms of the future is mostly concealed to us (Deuteronomy 29:29). I have no right to offer to people hopeful prognoses that have no biblical foundation. Salvation does not mean that all uncertainties have now been removed from the life of a believer, though many important uncertainties have. Of course, there are many certainties of the Christian faith. In 1 Corinthians 15:12–19, Paul lists a number of things that would be realities if Christ were not raised from the dead. For example, he says in verse 17, "if Christ has not been raised, your faith is futile and you are still in your sins." However, in verse 20, he states the reality of the resurrection: "But in fact Christ has been raised from the dead." My point is that we have many wonderful certainties that our faith is founded upon. Further, we have the certainty of God's faithfulness, so that we know what he promised, he will perform. These things make up the substance of our hope. We are to live with the understanding that our uncertainties are not God's uncertainties for he does not have uncertainties!

Hope has an actual and firm foundation. It is not simply having a positive outlook on life. I once read a story that might help here. I believe it was based on events that were true. I will tell it the way I remember it though I am a little sketchy about all of the details. It seems there was a high school football team in a part of the country where high school football is extremely popular. This particular team hadn't done very well for some years. They had lost a very significant number of games in a row. A new season came and people's *hopes* (the secular kind) were up. The first game was approaching and the owner of a local used car dealership asked if he could address the team. He promised each player a working used car if they won the game. The players, coaches, and fans were excited about the game. Perhaps the players had visions in their heads about the cars they would soon be driving. There were pep rallies, motivational speeches, confident attitudes, and more. At game time, human optimism for this team was as high as could be. Unfortunately, they got crushed. You see, the other team was simply far better at playing football than they were! Biblical hope is not human optimism. It is the certain expectation we have now about God's promises which are real. We do not have to invent promises. What we have in Christ is unfathomably great! How marvelous is the truth that our God is faithful! "Let us hold fast the confession of our hope without wavering, for he who promised is faithful" (Hebrews 10:23).

Hope in Christ Is Not Positive Thinking or Name It and Claim It

Though this point is similar to the first one, there is a difference. In positive thinking the idea is that thinking positively about something is what brings it about. The positive thinking is the decisive factor in making it happen. Biblical hope has nothing to do with this kind of thinking. It is not our thinking that brings something to pass. It is God's sovereign will. God has ordained that all of his good purposes be accomplished. He is God. He meticulously and exhaustively rules. In his word, there are several examples of a figure of speech called a *merism*. A merism involves a statement of polar extremes that, by implication, include all that come between them. Some verses, using merisms, imply then that all of life's events are comprehensively under God's control. Consider Deuteronomy 32:39: "See now that I, even I, am he, and there is no god beside me; I kill and I make alive; I wound and I heal; and there is none that can deliver out of my hand." When God says that he kills and makes alive, he is saying that he does these two things (the polar extremes) and everything between them as well. In other words, he controls life and death and all things in between! We find the same kind of thing in Isaiah 45:7: "I form light and create darkness, I make well-being and create calamity, I am the LORD, who does all these things." When God says that he forms light and creates darkness (again, the polar extremes), he is stating that he creates everything. When God says that he makes well-being and creates calamity (once again, the polar extremes), he is teaching us that he ordains all that comes to pass. We must understand that though there is no evil in God whatsoever, he is still sovereign over it. Nothing happens that does not come under the sovereignty of God. All that happens, happens according to God's good purposes. "In him we have obtained an inheritance, having been predestined according to the purpose of him who works all things according to the counsel of his will" (Ephesians 1:11).

Name it and claim it is similar to positive thinking. It is essentially thinking that one can pray their own will into reality. It involves expecting God to do that which he has not promised to do. That is not biblical hope. This concept is a contradiction to God's absolute sovereignty. It makes the "namer and claimer" the sovereign. It would mean that God has not ordained all of his good purposes to come about but has left some things in the hands of sinful humankind! Our hope and confidence is certainly not is ourselves. We are to submit ourselves to God. We are to pray with an attitude of embracing his sovereign good purposes as Jesus did in the Garden of Gethsemane: "Nevertheless, not as I will, but as you will" (Matthew 26:39). Our hope is in that which God has ordained, those things that he has ordained which have been revealed to us in his Word. We know that there is so much that God has not revealed to us, but that he has revealed to us all that we need to know to live life for his glory (Deuteronomy 29:29; 2 Peter 1:3).

Hope in Christ Is Not Arrogant Presumption

Hope is a humble characteristic. Though it involves a confident assurance in God's faithfulness, it is accompanied by a humble, dependent, and submissive posture. The object of our confidence is God and the means of our confidence is faith. However, this very same faith understands that the Spirit of God now works in our hearts to grow us in our knowledge of God and our pursuit of holiness. Hope does not take the presumptuous attitude that it no longer matters how one lives because God has promised to save us. We must understand that our salvation is from sin, not just its penalty. In 1 Peter, immediately after commanding believers to set their hope fully on the grace to be revealed at Christ's coming, Peter then commands the pursuit of holiness (1 Peter 1:13–16).

The arrogant presumption I am speaking of could be defined as *a carnal attitude absent of the fear of God that sees salvation as a rescue from the penalty of sin while at the same time allowing the rescued person to mock God with a life little concerned with that which greatly concerns God.* This is not the salvation the Scriptures reveal. Christian confidence is the confidence of those who have been born again. Christian salvation is a salvation that changes one's heart. Christian salvation includes the presence and sanctifying power of God's Spirit. In fact, it is God's indwelling Spirit that gives us confident assurance. "For you did not receive the spirit of slavery to fall back into fear, but you have received the Spirit of adoption as sons, by whom we cry, "Abba! Father!" The Spirit himself bears witness with our spirit that we are children of God" (Romans 8:15–16).

It is the Spirit of God who desires us to have the confident expectation that is called *hope*! Our doubt in God's faithfulness and promises would not glorify God. I recently read about a college chaplain who held, on the campus of the college he ministered at, what he called "a festival of doubt." The goal of this event was to support the importance of religious uncertainty. In other words, he upheld the philosophy that it was good to doubt one's faith. This is not really surprising as we live in a time in which the spirit of skepticism is considered a virtue. This is not the spirit that the Word of God pictures the believer as having. Those born again have a kind of birthright—confidence in God. As we have said, it is a dependent, humble kind of confidence, absolutely not in ourselves. Nonetheless, it is genuine assurance. God is faithful. We can believe God because we know he is real and true and has secured for us our salvation through Christ. God does not want us to celebrate uncertainty. He does not want us to wander around aimlessly in a fog of doubt. He wants us to have hope in abundance, but hope is not arrogant presumption!

So hope is not human optimism or positive thinking or arrogant presumption. It deals with matters of spiritual reality. It is not based on man's wisdom (our own or others) but God's grace through Jesus Christ. We look to God's redemptive work as recorded for us in God's Word. It is there we find a hope that is not matched by anything this world has to offer. Biblical hope is far, far greater than human substitutes. It is in this biblical hope we go forth and endure, for God's eternal joy has been set before us!

5

What Hope Embraces

We have made an attempt so far to define biblical hope and show that it is vitally important for the Christian life. In this chapter, we want to now show some of the distinct areas that are affected by our hope in Christ. Hope is engendered by certain realities of our Christian faith. As we embrace in our hearts these realities of our faith, joy and endurance become powerful features of our lives with which we run the Christian race. What hope embraces can be seen in four distinct frameworks.

Hope in Terms of Our Temporal Needs

We can be confident in God's continual provision for our material and physical needs for as long as we need them. We can rest securely today that tomorrow he will still be our loving Father who cares for and provides for his children. The apostle Peter tells us that in salvation we have "now returned to the Shepherd and Overseer of [our] souls" (1 Peter 2:25). This is the very Shepherd that David trusted in. Therefore, we can say with confidence, "The LORD is my shepherd; I shall not want" (Psalm 23:1). I love how Jesus explains God's loving provision in Matthew 7:11: "If you then, who are evil, know how to give good gifts to your children, how much more will your Father who is in heaven give good things to those who ask him!" Jesus is teaching God's provision in the context of prayer. He speaks of finite and fallen human fathers who still know how to give good gifts to their children. He actually speaks of human beings of being *evil*! This is the teaching of God's Word. Human beings, by nature, are not good. This is the very reason we have need to be saved. However, in spite of being evil, human fathers can still give good gifts to their children. With that in mind, Jesus says, "how much more" in terms of our heavenly Father. The idea is that our heavenly Father most certainly knows how to give good gifts to his children. He is certainly more willing and infinitely more able! So our hope even extends to a confident assurance that God will answer our prayers for real needs that we have! Just a chapter earlier in the gospel of Matthew, Jesus taught about the certainty of the Father's material provision. He taught that believers should not be anxious about material provision (Matthew 6:25). He reasoned that "if God so clothes the grass of the field, which today is alive and tomorrow is thrown into the oven, will he not much more clothe you, O you of little faith?" (Matthew 6:30). God's example in providing for the birds and clothing the fields with beauty points to the truth that God will provide material needs for his own children. Christ's point in the passage is that we must not be people of little faith. My point here is that it is this faith that is the substance of our hope. God will provide for any tomorrows that he gives me in this present age.

We must understand that the oldest lie in the history of mankind is this: "You cannot trust God"! Though it was not expressed in those words, it was the essence of what Satan said to Eve in the Garden of Eden. God had commanded that the fruit of the tree of the knowledge of good and evil was not to be eaten. When Satan came along to tempt Eve, she told him that God commanded them not to eat the fruit or touch it lest they die. Now, God never did say not to touch it, but he did day not to eat it for they would die if they did. Satan said to Eve: "You will not surely die. For God knows that when you eat of it your eyes will be opened and you will be like God, knowing good and evil" (Genesis 3:4–5). The implication of Satan's words to Eve is clear: God is holding back something that is good for you. God has even lied to you saying that you will die. You cannot trust God. Jesus said of Satan that "he was a murderer from the beginning, and has nothing to do with the truth, because there is no truth in him. When he lies, he speaks out of his own character, for he is a liar and the father of lies" (John 8:44). "You cannot trust God" is a really big lie. We are to be a people who believe God and trust God's truthfulness and faithfulness. He is God. He cannot lie (Titus 1:2; Hebrews 6:18). This faith in God brings forth the hope that God will continue to provide for me in terms of temporal needs.

This hope is further strengthened by another one of God's promises. Paul wrote in Philippians 4:19, "And my God will supply every need of yours according to his riches in glory in Christ Jesus." This verse is found toward the very end of the book of Philippians. It is connected to Paul's commendation of the Philippian church for their continued partnership in the gospel. They had sent him a gift to help with his material needs. Paul adds to his commendation the assurance and comforting truth that God will meet all of their real needs as well. God as their heavenly Father is the ultimate giver! Some say that this promise is only for those who support gospel missions. They believe that Paul is saying something like: "because you gave to missions to meet my needs, God will supply your needs." This makes the promise conditional and also an incentive to give to missions. The thinking for believers would be, "I better give to missions, because I sure do want my needs met!" I believe this is the wrong way to look at it. Paul is not saying, "Because you gave to me, God will meet your needs." Instead, Paul is explaining to them that they do not need to worry about the fact that they sacrificially gave, because God is our heavenly Father who meets all of our needs. Now, if a professing Christian is not a giver, is continually selfish, has no desire for the gospel to be spread for God's glory and the joy of human beings, has no desire to worship God in this way, then there are more serious things to worry about than just the idea that God may not meet his or her material needs. Perhaps the question might be for such a person: "Is he really your God?" Or, "Why do you not desire to be like him—loving and giving?" The bottom line is that this promise is not conditional but arises from the goodness and grace of our heavenly Father. It does motivate us in the sense that it frees our giving because we can trust God to supply our needs. However, the promise does not rely on us but on God's grace. In the promise, we can consider, then, the source: "my God." We must be sure we have the right God. Our God must be the God of Scripture, the living and true God, the Creator, the Redeemer. This is the God who shepherds his people so that they do not lack. There is also the *supply*: "according to his riches." Thus, it is a supply that knows no limit. God, of course, will never experience some kind of economic crisis or emergency situation. He is the almighty God. He does not have unlimited resources—he is the unlimited resource! We must also consider the *specifics* of the promise: "every need of yours." The idea is that God actually knows all of your needs. In all of what I have written so far about God meeting our needs, the key is that we are dealing with real needs. Only God knows perfectly what each of us need. He knows your material needs, and, beyond that, and more importantly, he knows your spiritual needs. God knows our need to know him and delight in him and desire him and be satisfied in him and glorify him. Further, he knows our need to be steadfast in our faith through our hope. This promise in Philippians 4:19 is actually way better than we could imagine. It is not about our own sometimes self-centered and manufactured felt needs. It is about what we need now as God continues to work in us to conform us in the image of his Son. It surely includes temporal provision unless God deems it necessary for a time to withhold that from us. In that case, and for that time, our temporal provision is not a need. I say this because in Philippians 4:12, right before Paul says that God will supply all needs, Paul speaks of "learning the secret of facing plenty and hunger, abundance and need." Paul was speaking of learning how to be content. Apparently, there were times when hunger was part of God's good purposes for Paul for a time. Yet, God obviously brought Paul through that time. Thus, our hope embraces God supplying our real needs including the temporal ones, even if for a time we face some paucity.

Hope in Terms of Our Spiritual Security

Biblical hope is all about confidence, security, and assurance. We discussed this a little bit in the last chapter as we thought about arrogant presumption as opposed to humble assurance. My point here is simply this: Christians ought to be those who do not simply have a wishful desire to have eternal life but those who know they have eternal life. "I write these things to you who believe in the name of the Son of God that you may know that you have eternal life" (1 John 5:13). We can be confident that our salvation is secure because we believe in the name of the Son of God.

First John 5:13 is a wonderful verse and it is worth exploring its context a little more here. It gives us one of the main reasons that John wrote this letter. John was addressing a situation in which some had left the churches because they were never true believers in the first place (1 John 2:19). Some have called these people *secessionists* because they seceded from the physical union with the body of Christ. John calls them *antichrists* because they had a false theology concerning the person of Christ. John writes 1 John against these false professors and for the true saints pointing to the confidence they can have in Christ. John is saying that God desires that his children know that eternal life is their present possession. God wants his genuine children to know and have confidence that he has saved them and is saving them and will saved them completely! We must understand that it is not enough to know that this verse speaks of having assurance of salvation. We must also know the "these things" that John has written about in this letter that are the basis of our assurance. Essentially, the "these things" are the substance of the letter. All through the letter of 1 John, John has been pointing out the marks of genuine Christianity. The letter is filled with many doctrinal and practical tests. These marks include: believers acknowledge their sins; believers love other believers; believers practice righteousness not lawlessness; believers have a sound Christology, recognizing that Jesus is the Christ, the Son of God, come in the flesh, come to shed his blood for sin. So 1 John 5:13 speaks of the confidence believers can have ("that you may know"), the object of that confidence ("the Son of God"), the agency God uses to connect us to the object ("believe"), and the ultimate goal of the confidence ("eternal life"). The marks of genuine Christianity are not meritorious works for only Christ's work merits our salvation. They are simply the fruit of God's work in us. Indeed, we take small steps toward Christ's likeness in this life. We dare not trust our works, whatsoever. As James 3:2 puts it, "We all stumble in many ways"! The presence of these marks, though very imperfect, allows our confidence to be strengthened but all the while our confidence is in Christ alone. We must see these works as the Spirit's work in us, and we must, at the same time, always see our salvation as something that comes from outside of us—Jesus Christ.

Christ is indeed the good shepherd who can never lose any of his true sheep (John 10:27–30). Thus, God wants his true sheep to be spiritually secure (not arrogantly presumptuous!), and this security certainly brings us true hope of eternal life. Paul explains that our faith brings forth this hope when he writes in Titus 1:2, "in hope of eternal life, which God, who never lies, promised before the ages began." Hope certainly encompasses our spiritual security. When it seems like all else is failing, Christ as our Redeemer, will never fail. he is indeed our blessed hope!

Hope in Terms of Our Sanctification and Endurance

We can also be confident that God will continue his work in us and give us grace to endure to the end. He will not let anything separate us from his love (Romans 8:31–39). Hope embraces this truth with joy. Every day God's mercies are fresh and new (Lamentations 3:22–23) and in all of life, his grace is sufficient (2 Corinthians 12:9). Interestingly enough, this hope I have for progress in my holiness shows up in some unusual ways. I believe we all have these episodes. Let me describe them in four parts.

We mourn over our sin

I have encountered some believers who do not think this is a good thing. They feel that we are saints who should not dwell on our sin at all. If that were the case, how could we confess it? How could we seek to put it to death? Believers should mourn over the brokenness of this world. Jesus taught this in Matthew 5:4 when he said: "Blessed are those who mourn, for they shall be comforted." We must certainly remember that we are part of the brokenness not its cure. Christ alone is Savior and he is quite sufficient for the task! Mourning for our brokenness is a blessed thing. The Greek word here for *blessed* is *makarios*.

Some would say it means *happy* but that is too light a word in our culture to describe the meaning in this context. This blessedness transcends the trivial and superficial happiness we are prone to speak of. The word speaks of a state or condition that sets the believer apart from the rest of the world as one has experienced the grace of God. It points to the very best way to experience life in God. Jesus is saying that mourning over the brokenness of sin in the world is the best way to live. This includes our own sin. I long for it to be done away with.

We cry out concerning our wretchedness

This is where our mourning sometimes takes us. Like Paul we exclaim "Wretched man (or woman) that I am! Who will deliver me from the body of this death?" (Romans 7:24). Again, contrary to our culture of self-glory, this is not a bad thing. I find myself agreeing with Charles Simeon on this matter. He was appointed to pastor Trinity Church in Cambridge, England in November of 1782 and stayed there 54 years until his death in November of 1836. When he first began his pastorate, the church members locked the pew doors on Sunday mornings and then during the Sunday evening lectures as well. They did not come to church and they also refused to let those who did come, sit in the pews. This situation lasted at intervals for at least ten years.[1] If nothing else, Simeon is the model for pastoral endurance in one church! But there is much more to this man. For our purposes however, let me move on to a quote

---

1. Handley Moule, *Charles Simeon* (Forgotten Books: 2012, originally published, 1892), 38–46

of Simeon's that caught my attention. Simeon said: "There are two objects that I have ever desired for these forty years to behold; the one, is my own vileness; and the other is, the glory of God in the face of Jesus Christ: and I have always thought that they should be viewed together; just as Aaron confessed all the sins of Israel whilst he put them on the head of the scapegoat. The disease did not keep him from applying to the remedy, nor did the remedy keep him from feeling the disease. By this I seek to be, not only humble and thankful but humbled in thankfulness, before my God and Savior continually."[2] Should we desire to contemplate our own vileness? Should we spend time thinking about our sinfulness? Some folks I know cringe at this prospect. They feel like the gospel is all about our self-affirmation. They do not seem understand human depravity. They see themselves as sinners saved by grace. That's a good thing. But they do not appear to see the depth of their sinfulness as revealed in the Scriptures. I know firsthand that some believers feel that contemplating one's sinfulness would be foolish. It would be very unhealthy for one's self-identity. I must confess I believe these kinds of thoughts are not coming from Scripture but from current worldly trends. So, I think that sometimes we must cry out to God concerning our falling short of his glory in our sinfulness. However, and this is important, we must not let this lead us to despair! (Remember, this is a book about *hope*.) These cries concerning our wretchedness must lead us to the cross! It is there that we find assurance of God's steadfast love and forgiveness. We find no condemnation but instead find peace and renewed hope. We look to Christ because he is our hope. Our remaining sin points us to grace received and to a faithful God who will finish what he began (Philippians 1:6). Hope keeps us plodding in our faith journey.

2. William Carcus, *Memoirs of the Life of the Rev. Charles Simeon* (London: 1847), 303,304, quoted in John Piper, *The Roots of Endurance* (Illinois: Crossway, 2002), 108

We look to Christ

AS Paul cries out "Who will deliver me from this body of death?" in Romans 7:24, he also answers his own question in verse 25, "Thanks be to God through Jesus Christ our Lord!" As those who confess our sins, we also recognize that Christ is our advocate before the throne. In 1 John 2:1 we read: "My little children, I am writing these things to you so that you may not sin. But if anyone does sin, we have an advocate with the Father, Jesus Christ the righteous." This verse contains such glorious truth. Jesus is always the answer when it comes to our personal sin. "If anyone sins" presupposes that we will. The word *advocate* here is extremely significant. The NIV helpfully paraphrases it "one who speaks in our defense." The Greek word is *parakletos* and is only used by John in the New Testament. Four times in the gospel of John, this word refers to the Holy Spirit who comes to testify concerning Jesus. However, here in 1 John 2:1, it refers to Jesus Christ who speaks on our behalf to the Father when we sin. The basic meaning of the word is *helper*. It is paired here with the words *the Father* to convey the truth that Jesus helps us with our sin before the Father. A technical, theological definition of Christ's advocacy goes something like this: *Christ constantly secures our acceptance with God and God's favor with us. he is maintaining a constant acquittal of our sins before God. He represents us on the basis of his finished work.* So, Jesus is our defense attorney. And he wins for us all the time! He advocates for us continually, perfectly, and freely. Paul pictures how this works in Romans 8:31–34: "What then shall we say to these things? If God is for us, who can be against us? He who did not spare his own Son but gave him up for us all, how will he not also with him graciously give us all things? Who shall bring any charge against God's elect? It is God who justifies. Who is to condemn? Christ Jesus is the one who died—more than that, who was raised—who is at the right hand of God, who indeed is interceding for us." Let me explain these verses.

In this kind of courtroom scenario, God is for us because our judge is actually now our heavenly Father. It is our judge who went through unfathomable lengths to get us out from condemnation. Any charges brought before the judge are not going to hold up because God our Father is the one who decides our case, no one else! Every accusation ends the same way—*not guilty*—because our advocate pleads for us continually and the Father accepts the Son, is pleased with the Son, and accepts the Son's atoning work on our behalf. For genuine believers, the following two truths must be understood. First, as long as Jesus is advocating for us before the throne with the Father, we will never be, we never can be condemned for our sins. Second, his advocacy has a practical effect on our relationship with the Father when we sin. The Father continues to favor us or bless us in Christ. Now, this may include at times loving discipline, but it is loving. Because of Christ's advocacy, his Fatherly care can never cease. Jesus our advocate secures all of our blessings. So, we look to Christ.

We find refreshment in the gospel
(and our hope is renewed)

Because of the above, we find refreshment in the glorious gospel. On the basis of his cross, Christ is still working on our behalf. We are truly secure as Hebrews 7:25 says, "He is able to save to the uttermost those who draw near to God through him, since he always lives to make intercession for them." God indeed continues to pour out his grace upon us. Our souls are continually refreshed in Jesus Christ. I can have confident assurance that Christ is my security. I can have confident assurance that I am being kept by the power of God to an inheritance that is, as 1 Peter 1:4 puts it, "imperishable, undefiled, and unfading."

Hope in Terms of Resurrection and the
Fullness of God's Kingdom

Here now we have the ultimate hope. All of God's redemptive promises consummated. We can be confident that Jesus will return for us and bring us into the fullness of his kingdom where God will dwell with his people and his people will worship him with joy evermore. This is why we look for the blessed hope and glorious appearing of our God and Savior Jesus Christ (Titus 2:13). How we should expectantly await the day when Christ makes all things new and there will be no more sin, death, suffering, or sorrow. Most importantly, we will be in the presence of our glorious God as his chosen and holy and beloved. How we will forever praise the glorious grace of God we have in Jesus Christ! We will have no more sin. We will be able to love God with all of our hearts, souls, and minds. This fullness of the kingdom is where our hope must surely be fixed upon even now (1 Peter 1:13).

Let me close this chapter with an account of John Newton's last recorded words. A young pastor in London in 1807 named William Jay paid a visit to John Newton as his health and memory were rapidly deteriorating. Newton was Jay's pastoral mentor and Jay brought a notebook with him on the visit. Newton died a few weeks after this visit. Jay had only jotted down a single line from this last visit with Newton. It read, "My memory is nearly gone, but I remember two things: that I am a great sinner and that Christ is a great Savior."[3] Our hope embraces some glorious truths all grounded in our great Savior!

3. Jonathan Aitken, John Newton: From Disgrace to Amazing Grace (Crossway: Illinois, 2007), 347

6

The Enemies of Hope

We have defined biblical hope as the joyful and confident expectation of all the future fulfillment of redemptive promises for those in Christ. We experience this hope in the present. Our hearts rejoice in the greatness of all that God has done (this brings forth thanksgiving) and our hearts rejoice in all that God has promised he will do because of Christ (this is what hope does). Though all of this is a vital part of the Christian life, it does not negate the reality of struggle. Every believer is in the midst of spiritual warfare. The good news is that we fight the battle from the position of certain victory. In fact, the victory has already been won by Christ. The enemy has already been defeated and dethroned. Nonetheless, it is also true that sometimes God's children seem to be barely hanging on. We live in the tension of the already and the not yet. We have already been brought into the kingdom of Christ (Colossians 1:13). Christ is already ruling as the conquering Messiah-King (Matthew 28:18). But the fullness of the kingdom has not yet come. Thus, in the meantime, we must endure hardness as good soldiers and fight the fight of faith until the time of our departure or the coming of Christ.

All of this means that it is a reality that hope can be very weak in one's heart at times. As believers, we can never fully lose hope because we can never fully lose faith. Though we can have episodes of great weakness, Christ is making intercession for us so that our faith will not fail. Here is how Jesus explained this to Peter in Luke 22:31–32: "Simon, Simon, behold, Satan demanded to have you, that he might sift you like wheat, but I have prayed for you that your faith may not fail. And when you have turned again, strengthen your brothers." Later Peter is able to write to the saints about how God will test our faith for genuineness but not so it will fail, but so it will be found genuine to the praise, glory, and honor of Christ (1 Peter 1:6–7).

In this chapter, then, we want to examine some of the enemies of gospel hope and look at the ways we must fight for it. Though Christ makes intercession so that neither our faith nor our hope will ultimately fail, God uses means for victory in these areas. These means certainly include our being aware of the enemies of hope and our use of God-appointed ways to fight for it.

Let's begin by looking at a working definition that encompasses all of the enemies of hope: *Anything that causes the Christian to take his/her eyes off of Jesus Christ and the hope-giving grace that comes by way of the gospel is the enemy of hope.* We need God to continually comfort our hearts through Christ. God gives us eternal comfort and hope through grace. 2 Thessalonians 16:17 puts it this way: "Now may our Lord Jesus Christ himself, and God our Father, who loved us and gave us eternal comfort and good hope through grace, comfort your hearts and establish them in every good work and word." God comforts our hearts and fills them with hope by grace. Paul tells Timothy in 2 Timothy 2:1 to be "strengthened by the grace that is in Christ Jesus." The writer of Hebrews warns against seeking spiritual strength through legalistic practices and affirms in Hebrews 13:9 that it is "good for the heart to be strengthened by grace." So, as we examine several enemies of hope, we must understand what makes them enemies is that they tempt us to look away from the gospel—to look away from Christ who is our life! We will consider five such enemies of hope and then we will examine ways we must fight against these enemies.

Discouragement

We can get discouraged when relationships, work, ministry, and all the other aspects of our lives do not go the way we desired them to go. Sometimes, that discouragement can be strong and overwhelming. We see this in David's cries in Psalm 143:3–4: "For the enemy has pursued my soul; he has crushed my life to the ground; he has made me sit in darkness like those long dead. Therefore my spirit faints within me; my heart within me is appalled." In verse 7 of the same Psalm, David prays for a quick answer to his pleas for help: "Answer me quickly, O LORD! My spirit fails!" David is certainly overwhelmed. Yet, as the Psalm unfolds, David seems to make this plea knowing deep down in his soul the steadfast love of God. My point is that discouragement tempts us to lose faith in God's steadfast love. It tempts us to take our eyes of Christ and his great grace that we receive on the basis of the cross.

Fear

In the midst of frightening circumstances, sometimes fear seems to be winning out over faith. In Mark 4:36–41, we find the first disciples frightened as they were in a boat on the sea in the midst of a great storm, while Jesus was in the stern asleep! They wake Jesus up and say to him, "Do you not care that we are perishing?" Jesus then proceeds to calm the storm. He then rebukes them for their lack of faith. Our faith can indeed be very weak at times. When faith is weak, it follows that hope is weak as well. Fear can paralyze us. Our eyes are focused on that which causes us to fear and we seem to forget that our God is faithful. Our joy flees and our immediate view is on impending danger. Fear is an enemy of hope.

Sorrow

The reality of life in this present evil age is that bad things happen to us and to those we love. Sometimes we hear people who question why bad things happen to good people. The problem with that question is that the focus of amazement is skewed. We should not be amazed that bad things happen to good people because in reality there are no good people from God's sovereign and perfect perspective. We are all sinners. The world is under God's just curse. We should actually be amazed that good things happen at all. But by God's common grace, good things happen all the time. Many sinful people enjoy many things in this life on a regular basis. God's goodness is given that they may at some point repent of sin. The bottom line here is that sorrow is part of this fallen world. Thus, believers will experience sorrowful events.

Sorrow becomes an enemy of hope when it overwhelms the believer and drowns out our joy in Christ. Sorrow and joy can exist at the same time in a Christian's heart. Oftentimes, however, the sorrow seems so crushing. We can forget that God has his good purposes even in these sorrowful circumstances. We have a difficult time on occasion remembering that the God who ordains that sorrows come our way is also the God of all comfort (2 Corinthians 1:3).

Spiritual Ignorance

This is a significant enemy. When we are not growing in the knowledge and understanding of the gospel, uncertainty and doubt can creep in and diminish our hope. In Ephesians 1:18, Paul is sharing how he prays for the Ephesians to grow spiritually. Part of his prayer for them is that their hearts might be enlightened so that they will "know what is the hope to which [God] has called [them]" and he further describes that hope as "the riches of his glorious inheritance in the saints." We will not know these things as we ought if we are not learning his word and growing in grace.

Pride

When we move in the direction of self-confidence as opposed to humble dependence, our hope shifts away from the gospel and moves in the direction of self-manufactured hope. This kind of hope is fictitious. It is an illusion. If we hope in ourselves, we are deluded. We are incapable of saving ourselves. I recently preached a series of expository messages through the book of Ecclesiastes. One of the most important truths in that book is that human beings are on a search for a kind of self-significance that cannot be achieved. Right from the beginning, the *preacher* in Ecclesiastes makes it clear that all of man's labor will not bring about a significant change to this present evil age. As David Gibson puts it, "Ecclesiastes is a meditation on how life seems to elude our grasp in terms of lasting significance."[1] Ecclesiastes 1:2 says that "all is vanity." *Vanity* in this verse does not mean *meaningless* but that life is fleeting. Ecclesiastes points to the reality that our lives are fleeting to the point that one cannot actually make a permanent impact on the whole. Thus following the statement about vanity is the question in verse 3: "What does man gain by all the toil at which he toils under the sun?" The obviously implied answer is that man's toil is vanity. Ecclesiastes involves a complex but unified argument that basically says that in this fallen and finite world, you and I will not be the savior. The good news is that God has provided *the* Savior! I call this truth "the Ecclesiastes Principle." Let me summarize it: fallen and finite human beings live fleeting lives such that their labors will not save the world, nor were they meant to. In other words, we must leave the saving to God! When all is said and done, after we are gone, the world will still be fallen, the present age will still be evil, and we will have changed no one's heart. We finite and fallen human beings cannot fix the brokenness of the world, only Christ can. This, of course, doesn't mean that we are passive. It doesn't mean that God cannot use us as means. It does mean that there is no room for pride. For our purposes here, it means that there is no room for hope in ourselves! As Proverbs 26:12 puts it, "Do you see a man who is wise in his own eyes? There is more hope for a fool than for him." Pride is an enemy of biblical hope because it shifts away from Christ to ourselves.

1. David Gibson, *Living Life Backwards: How Ecclesiastes Teaches Us to Live in Light of the End* (Illinois: Crossway, 2017), 21

Fighting Against the Enemies of Hope

Now that we have looked at some of the enemies of hope, let us look at some practical ways we can fight for hope. Please remember that in all of these ways, the goal is keeping our eyes on Jesus Christ. As Hebrews 12:1–2 tell us, we must run the Christian race with endurance "looking to Jesus, the founder and perfecter of our faith." First of all, we must have it firmly fixed in our hearts that we cannot place our hope in anything else but Christ, for anything but Christ is unreliable and false in terms of hope. I love Psalm 33: 16–17: "The king is not saved by his great army; a warrior is not delivered by his great strength. The war horse is a false hope for salvation, and by its great might it cannot rescue." These verses simply affirm the fact that although some things may seem strong and mighty and powerful, they cannot save anyone's soul. Only Christ provides forgiveness of sin and reconciliation to God. He is our hope.

Secondly, it is important to be encouraged in the gospel each and every day. We dare not stand in our own strength for a moment. When discouragement comes upon us, we must find relief in the glorious gospel. I was brought up in a legalistic kind of Christianity. This lends itself to a self-righteousness and self-dependency. I would wake up in the morning and see the need to perform for God in order to earn his favor. I am ashamed to say that I actually thought on some days that I had succeeded. As time went on, God graciously grew me in the faith and showed me the foolishness of moving away from the gospel into a performance-based Christian lifestyle. I no longer start my day with a performance-oriented posture before God. Again, God most graciously showed me that I could never earn his favor by some kind of self-performance. God is pleased with his work for his work alone is perfect. So instead of days beginning with the thought of self-performance, I do just the opposite. I wake up and immediately acknowledge that I need mercies fresh and new, and need enabling grace to function for the day. I also recognize that these mercies and grace are mine because of Christ alone! We must continually spend time reviewing the meaning and significance of the gospel. Though the word of the cross is foolishness to the unsaved, "to us who are being saved it is the power of God" (1 Corinthians 1:18).

In the third place, we can fight for hope by looking in Scripture continually to see the faithfulness of God. As we read of God's faithfulness through the redemptive story, and as we see specific didactic (teaching) passages that explain this faithfulness and steadfast love, we are letting the Word of God encourage our hearts and strengthen our hope. There are so many places in Scripture that point out to us God's faithfulness. For example, in Philippians 1:6 Paul says, "And I am sure of this, that he who began a good work in you will bring it to completion at the day of Jesus Christ." David beautifully expresses God's faithfulness in Psalm 57:10: "For your steadfast love is great to the heavens, your faithfulness to the clouds." Do not neglect the Word of God as you fight for gospel hope.

Fourth and finally, do not neglect the local church and fellowship with other believers, but instead cultivate a fellowship of encouragement in the local church. God has ordained the local church as a means of grace. The church does not save, Jesus saves. However, that does not neglect the truth that God uses the church as a means of endurance for the saints. It is critically important to be connected to a proper local body of believers. Although Hebrews 10:23–25 may be familiar, the truths in these verses never get old: "Let us hold fast the confession of our hope without wavering, for he who promised is faithful. And let us consider how to stir up one another to love and good works, not neglecting to meet together, as is the habit of some, but encouraging one another, and all the more as you see the Day drawing near." I was once told by a young believer that he was seriously considering making the campus ministry at his college his local church. I asked him a few questions. "Does this ministry do baptisms? Do you observe the Lord's Supper there? Do they practice church discipline? Are the leaders ordained and considered pastors?" He replied "No" to all of these questions. I then told him that he could not make this ministry his local church because it was not a local church! Every believer, if at all possible, needs to sit under the preaching and teaching of God's Word with a body of believers assembled as a church body. Every believer needs all of the various ordinary means of grace that a local church administrates. This certainly includes simply being among faithful believers who can encourage one another in the faith. Fight for hope by assembling with brothers and sisters in Christ in a local congregation. Participate in the true fellowship of God's people. You cannot expect spiritual encouragement from the world, but you should find it among the people of God.

The Christian life is always a life that humbly looks outward to God. The great enemies of hope are those things that tempt you to look anywhere else. Praise God that he is faithful. Jesus, at this very moment, is praying for your faith to endure. He will not leave you and he will not abandon you. If God is for you, discouragement, fear, sorrow, spiritual ignorance, and pride cannot ultimately win. Jesus wins—and we win in him.

7

Letting Go of Hopes That Are Not God-Centered

As I have said, hope is a present experience in light of future certainty. It is the joyful and confident expectation of all of the future fulfillment of God's redemptive promises for those in Jesus Christ. Our hope is secure because the future fullness of God's redemptive work is based on what Christ merited not what we merit. Hope is secure because God is pleased with his Son and his redemptive work! In the previous chapter we looked at the enemies of hope and how we should fight for hope. In this chapter, I want to call attention to the fact that there is a need for us to relinquish hopes that are not God-centered. The hopes I am now speaking about involve our own personal wishes, dreams, ambitions, goals, and desires. We must look to God and his good purposes and willingly, gladly embrace them.

Understanding the Realm Shift

We previously mentioned the *realm shift* in the first chapter. Let's look a little closer at this biblical concept. It is, as we formerly stated, based on Colossians 1:13 which says, "he has delivered us from the domain of darkness and transferred us to the kingdom of his beloved Son." In salvation, we have been moved to a new realm so to speak. We have been taken out of the realm of darkness and brought into the realm of Christ. A real realm shift has been brought about in Christ. *Shift* can be defined as a transfer or movement from one place to another. *Realm* is a domain or area ruled by something. In the first chapter, I gave the example of the kitchen being my wife's domain. My culinary skills consist of making mac and cheese from a package. I can also grill a hot dog on the stove. Thus, when my wife, whose culinary skills far surpass mine, prepares one of her special dishes, it is understood that I stay away. It is her domain (even though I just want to help, honest!). Colossians is speaking about a transfer from one kingdom to another. However, since it is not a physical kingdom yet, *realm* would certainly be an appropriate word. Well, we have been brought into Jesus' realm! And the implications are huge. It is extremely important that you understand, if you are a Christian, that you are no longer on the journey of self. As a believer, it must now be God's purposes that are important. You have been made new in Christ and indwelt by his Spirit. This newness now shapes what our goals should be. Simply put, our goals should be God's will. This means God's will in terms of what he has prescribed in his Word, and, also, his will in terms of what he is actually going to do in this world. Our new realm existence changes everything. We have new attitudes, behaviors, and (you guessed it) hopes. These should also shape our prayers. They should bring forth worship, praise, thanksgiving, reverence, and awe toward God. The new realm is where we live. It is important not to confuse the *American dream* with God's kingdom purposes. This new realm is all about God's glory. It is about Christ and our being brought into a relationship with him such that we know his glory and rejoice in him. Thus, Colossians 1:27 says that it has been made known to believers "the riches of the glory of this mystery, which is Christ in you, the hope of glory." The gospel has been revealed fully to us and included in that revelation is our appearance with Christ in glory (Colossians 3:4). The phrase "Christ in you, the hope of glory" could be paraphrased "Christ is in you giving you assurance of experiencing the presence of his glory." Here is a hope worth waiting for! Someday, believers will be in the presence of Jesus Christ beholding his glory. The Christian life must not be reduced to Jesus as a helper, life-coach, or problem-solver. Though he certainly is our help and guide, and solves many of our problems, the Christian life involves a real kingdom shift which brings about Christ-centered desires—new goals and values. We must relinquish the hopes of the old realm for the glorious hope of the new.

The Call to Let Go of Selfish Hopes

In Christ's call to follow him, we find these words in Luke 9:23: "And he said to all, 'If anyone would come after me, let him deny himself and take up his cross daily and follow me.'" This self-denial refers to a denial of all of the old life. It involves the putting to death of sin, the renewal of our minds, the putting on of Christ, the letting go of all that is self-centered. In days gone by people used to speak of a *disinterested* love. By that was meant loving without one's self-interest driving that love. *Disinterested* did not mean one was not interested. It meant one was acting in a loving way without being motivated by any kind of self-glorifying gain. Well, Jesus calls his disciples to be disinterested in terms of self-glory. Another way of saying this is that our desires should match God's desires. James 4:3 speaks of a prayer life void of disinterest (in other words, filled with carnal interests): "You ask and do not receive, because you ask wrongly, to spend it on your passions." Our hope is a humble hope that involves looking forward to increasing joy in God not self. It involves a recognition that our future pleasure involves worshipping God. We ought now to find pleasure in worship. It ought to be growing. And we should be looking forward to the day when our worship is pure and our joy is full as we cry out that all glory, praise, and honor belong to God. Hope does not include future self-glory as the psalmist teaches us: "Not to us, O LORD, not to us, but to your name give glory, for the sake of your steadfast love and your faithfulness!" (Psalm 115:1). Man-centered hopes are flawed in some way, shape, or form. They do not come from a desire that God be glorified, but that man be satisfied in something man was never created to be satisfied with.

We Must Let Go of the Deceitful Concepts of What a Joyful Life Looks Like

Human beings are so mistaken about where true blessedness is to be found. Even believers are still susceptible to deceptions about this. We might think that a joyful life right now means that we have no suffering, no problems, no difficulties at work, no affliction, no pain, and more. Yet, we should know that in this life God uses these things for our good. Our weaknesses allow him to show forth his strength. It is obviously not that we relish suffering but rather that we are willing to embrace God's sovereign will and use it to strengthen our faith and grow us (Romans 8:28; 2 Corinthians 12:9–10). We may even sometimes envy those who lead sinful lives and seem to be enjoying the pleasures of sin. It is certainly helpful to know that the Scriptures inform us that these so-called pleasures are only for a season. Pointing out Moses choice to follow Yahweh, the God of his ancestors, Hebrews 11:25–26 says about him that when he was grown "he refused to be called Pharaoh's daughter, choosing rather to be mistreated with the people of God than to enjoy the fleeting pleasures of sin. He considered the reproach of Christ greater wealth than the treasures of Egypt, for he was looking to the reward." Moses had his eyes on the promises of God and not what the false gods of Egypt could offer. Like Moses, we are called to let go of the deceitful treasures this world system offers, and look to our true hope, Jesus Christ.

Do Not Love the World

I feel like it would be good at this point to look a little deeper at how important it is to treasure what is really proper to treasure and to let go of that which is not God-centered. To do this we turn to 1 John 2:15–17: "Do not love the world or the things in the world. If anyone loves the world, the love of the Father is not in him. For all that is in the world- the desires of the flesh and the desires of the eyes and pride of life—is not from the Father but is from the world. And the world is passing away along with its desires, but whoever does the will of God abides forever." There are five very important truths to consider here.

Believers Are Not to Love the Realm of Evil Sometimes Called *the World*

Here is the key command in this section, and it seems to be in two parts. First, do not love the world. The verb is a present imperative, indicating that not loving the world should be a continual lifestyle type of attitude. While the command in the Scriptures to love brothers and sisters in Christ implies a love of concern for another's well-being, the love here refers to the pleasure and gratification one receives from an object. It is like saying, "I love football" or "I love chocolate fudge" or like saying "I don't love broccoli" or "I don't love watching reality television." Here, it is "don't love the world." It means do not love the improper pleasure and gratification that the world brings. In other words, don't love the world because it doesn't bring proper pleasure and gratification.

To understand this command we must define the word *world* as used in this context. How can it be that God so loved the world, and that we are commanded not to love the world? It is because in the Scriptures this word *world* can be used in many ways. In John 3:16 it means the realm of humanity ("God so loved the world"—all humanity without distinction). In John 17:5 it means the entire universe or the physical earth ("And now, Father, glorify me in your own presence with the glory that I has with you before the world existed."—before the universe was created). In John 15:18 it means all humanity minus believers ("If the world hates you, you know it hated me before it hated you"—the unbelievers who, by nature, hate Christ). In John 4:42 It means Jews and Gentiles ("They said to the woman, 'It is no longer because of what you said that we believe, for we have heard for ourselves, and we know that this is indeed the Savior of the world.'"—the Savior of both Jews and

Gentiles not just Jews). So this word can be used in many ways, but in 1 John 2:15–17 it refers to the evil world system. It is what Paul refers to in Galatians 1:3 as this "present evil age." Essentially, John is saying do not love the values, attitudes, actions, philosophies, and behaviors that are opposed to God that we find embedded in the world of unbelief. James uses it in the same way in James 4:4: "You adulterous people, don't you know that friendship with the world is hatred toward God? Anyone who chooses to be a friend of the world becomes an enemy of God." Paul command in Romans 12:2 that we be not conformed to the world but that instead we be transformed by having our minds renewed in Christ. So John here does not mean "Do not love the created, physical world." Also, John does not mean "Do not love the world of humanity." John means do not love this system of evil that Satan himself rules over; a system that is completely anti-God in its philosophy and its deeds.

The second part of the imperative follows immediately: "or the things in the world." John does not mean don't love clouds or the ocean or ice-cream. He means don't love sin in all of its forms. Do not love the world as a whole (the system) and do not love the parts that make up the whole (the specific parts of the system). Don't love the specific evil anti-God attitudes and actions of the world system that rejects Christ. The world that has abandoned the creator and is voluntarily under control of the evil one because it refuses God's rule.

Believers Cannot Waiver between Holiness and Worldliness

John follows the imperative with a statement about one who would love the world of evil. Basically, he says that if you love the world of evil, then the love of the Father is not in you. This is not so hard to understand. One either loves sin or one loves God. John's point here is that it cannot be both. You are either born of God and the love of the Father is in your heart (meaning that because he loves you, you love him in response) or your affections are still strongly gravitating toward the sinful things of this evil world system and you do not love him. You cannot have it both ways; you cannot walk a tightrope between holiness and worldliness. In the Old Testament, Elijah told the children of Israel in his showdown with the false prophets of Baal on Mount Carmel that they must choose who they served: Baal (the false god Israel had been worshipping) or Yahweh (the living and true God). Elijah basically said you cannot serve both. If Yahweh is God then follow him, if Baal, then follow him. Jesus put it this way in Matthew 6:24, "No one can serve two masters, for either he will hate the one and love the other, or he will be devoted to the one and despise the other. You cannot serve God and money." Implied here is that genuine believers are the object of God's saving love. He gave his Son. Jesus died in our place on the cross. It is because of this we have love in our hearts for God and because of that for others. This is so much more satisfying that anything and everything that the evil realm can offer. So we are not to waiver. Instead we are to seek to grow in holiness which includes true happiness, not worldliness and the counterfeit happiness it offers.

Believers Must Understand That Although the Realm of Evil Is a Reality, It Is Not from God

Now John paints us a picture of what the essence of the worldly person is. What does a worldly person look like? Think like? What is worldliness? John says it consists of three things which all tie together: the "desires of the flesh," the "desires of the eyes," and the "pride of life." The first one ("desires of the flesh") appears to be the major category followed by two sub-categories. John specifically states that these three things are not from the Father but from the world. The Father did not create this evil world system although he did ordain that it come into being, for he is a sovereign God who has his good purposes for all things. The Father does not make anyone sin nor does he tempt anyone to sin. It is important to make the distinction here between God being sovereign over all yet not creating evil. For God has no evil in him. He permits it, and he is in control of it so that it can never extend beyond his sovereign bounds, and he even uses it to accomplish his good intentions, but it is not from him. God is perfectly holy. He is morally pure. He has no sin. Evil's origin is a mystery. We know it is a result of the fall (first of Satan, then of man). We know that those who partake in it will be judged (believers sins are judged on Calvary; the lost will be judged and condemned to hell at the end of the age). We know that God's righteousness will be shown to all. Though we cannot fully comprehend its origin, we surely can apprehend that it is a part of the reality of our planet and we are not to love it.

Believers Must Understand That One's Worldliness Comes from a Worldly Heart

Now, let's look a little closer to the three parts of the world as John describes them. First, we see the "desires of the flesh." In other words, right from the human heart, sinful worldliness pours out. John doesn't begin with the externals. He doesn't say, "all that is in the world," and then list things like pornography, sexual immorality, materialism, abortion, homosexuality, and so on. Instead, John points to the sinful desires that are inside the heart. In other words, to John, the first place we find worldliness is in ourselves! Sin is in the world in a specific way—it is in us. We take good things and make them bad: food is good—gluttony is sin; physical intimacy between husband and wife is good—pornography and sexual immorality is wicked; having shelter and clothing is good—making houses and clothes and material possessions one's god is a great, great evil. As Christians, we are being transformed by God's Spirit away from sin. Nonetheless, there is remaining sin in our hearts, and we must heed this admonition to love not the world. In spite of the transforming work of the Spirit, we cannot ignore the command here. It is for us and it is to be heeded, by the grace of God. John Calvin called the human heart an idol factory! We must be careful to treasure God and the good gifts he gives us because they are from him.

So John first points to worldliness within us. Then, he points to the "desires of the eyes." This refers to the fact that the human heart is incited to evil many times by what we see. We look without and it prompts our hearts to lust after it or desire it in a wrong way. It is not a sin to look at my neighbor's car, but the sight of it can provoke my heart to envy, anger, and bitterness. It is not a sin for a man to look at his neighbor's wife, but it is most certainly a sin to covet her. It violates the tenth commandment. The problem is that the eyes (what we see) drive us to sinful thoughts and actions. Back in Eden, as Satan enticed Eve, her eyes examined the fruit of the tree of the knowledge of good and evil. She took the fruit and ate. Worldliness comes from within and is inflamed in us from without by what we see.

Next, John points to the "pride of life." It points to the fact that we human beings have a desire to boast in a way that makes much of ourselves. Because of indwelling sin (our sin nature), normal self-love has become self-glory. We want to boast and be boasted about. Our desire is to be great, to be our own little gods. In fact, we actually think that for someone to love us, they must continually make much of us. We confuse love with worship. I think it was a Garfield comic I once saw where Garfield is saying "I'm tired of talking about myself; you talk about me for a while"! Instead, the gospel calls for a kind of self-forgetfulness because we find our satisfaction in praising and worshipping God. He is our supreme treasure. Paul exclaimed in Galatians 6:14, "But far be it from me to boast except in the cross of our Lord Jesus Christ, by which the world has been crucified to me, and I to the world." So with our focus on Jesus, we have no need to focus on ourselves, and we can spend time focusing on the needs of others. But worldliness happens because we want to boast in ourselves or our possessions or our achievements or our prestige. Worldliness comes from our hearts. We must praise God that we are not who we once were. We must also, rather than be presumptuous, look to the Word of God as a means God uses to transform us more and more. We must, by grace, seek to heed this warning.

Believers Must Understand That It Is God's Kingdom That Abides Not This Present Evil Age

The last thing John says about the evil world system is important: it is passing away along with its desires. The passing away of this present evil age is a process. Light has broken in on the darkness in a real and significant way. In fact, it has broken through in the greatest way possible, in Jesus Christ. The world (the evil system) will come to an end. As one believer put it, "there is no future in worldliness"!

What is lasting, or what abides forever (as John puts it here) are those who do the will of God. John uses this phrase, "whoever does the will of God," to primarily refer those who put their trust in Jesus Christ. As Jesus said in John 6:40, "For this is the will of my Father, that everyone who looks on the Son and believes in him should have eternal life, and I will raise him up on the last day." God's kingdom consists of God's people in God's appointed place humbly doing God's will and experiencing God's presence and blessings forever. This is what abides (really *who* abides)—God's people, and they abide forever. By grace they are saved, so there is no boasting, but there is eternal joy as someday sin is completely removed. So we must let go of the deceitful concepts of what a joyful life is and set our hopes fully on Christ!

The Hope We Are Called to Is Ultimately God-Glorifying and Eternally Satisfying

A hope-filled life involves replacing man-centered, finite, little thoughts with great thoughts about our great God. Peter says in 1 Peter 1:3 that we have been "born again to a living hope through the resurrection of Jesus Christ from the dead." Our hope is a living hope, meaning that it is a hope that is real, not imagined. We have a hope that has vitality, not emptiness and deadness. We have a hope in a resurrected Savior not a dead one. What hope can come from the current materialistic and naturalistic worldviews? All they can say is something like "eat, drink, and be merry for tomorrow we die!" Believers have a hope with substance. This hope drives us on; this hope keeps us going; this hope is alive right now in our hearts. This is God-centered hope. Let us let go of self-centered and deceitful hopes offered by the very world system that we are commanded not to love. Holding on to sinful temporal treasures is a denial of one's faith in the realities of eternal glory, the glory of God himself. We must let go of that which we could actually never keep, and more and more desire that for which we were actually created.

8

When Hope Joyfully Sings

Biblical hope produces joy. In this chapter I am going to focus on that joy. Though hope sustains us through difficult times, hope also is joyous. It may be quite difficult for us to comprehend this biblical truth, but it is an important one: sorrow and joy can simultaneously abide in the Christian's heart. As has been previously pointed out, biblical hope looks forward to kingdom promises. The working definition of hope I gave states that "hope is the joyful and confident expectation of the fulfillment of God's redemptive promises." Remember that God's kingdom has already broken into this present evil age in such a way that we are living in the realm of God's kingdom right now even as we await its fullness. Romans 14:17 states three of the outstanding characteristics of Christ's kingdom: righteousness, peace, and joy in the Holy Spirit. So it is proper to think carefully concerning the *joy* aspect of our *joyful* hope. In the midst of sorrow, we must understand that sorrow does not destroy the joy that our hope in Christ brings forth. This chapter will begin with a brief examination of the kind of joy biblical hope produces. Then move on to consider the fact that this kind of hope joyfully sings from the heart the praises of our God. Finally, I will stress the importance of praising God with songs that have Christ at the center.

A Hope-Filled Life

The Joy Biblical Hope Produces

The joy biblical hope produces is a joy that unrepentant sinners cannot experience. Proverbs 10:28 states: "The hope of the righteous brings joy, but the expectation of the wicked will perish." Those who know Christ are to know a joy inexpressible and filled with glory (1 Peter 1:8). This joy is a great gladness of heart that results as we know and treasure God properly. It grows as we know and treasure God more and more. It grows as our hope grows in abundance. Our joy says something about our God. The Psalmist says that "in [his] presence there is fullness of joy; at [his] right hand are pleasures forevermore" (Psalm 16:11). When a professing Christian lacks joy, it shows a lack of satisfaction in God. How can we not rejoice in the Lord always (Philippians 4:4)? We joy because the God we have communion with is a God full of joy. Hope produces joy as we grow in our recognition that Christ has risen and overcome all of our enemies (John 16:22–23; Colossians 2:15). Hope produces joy as we recognize that our heavenly Father hears and desires to answer our prayers (John 16:24). There is a settled joy in a believer's heart because God's love is steadfast and he is faithful. Every believer should seek to cultivate this joy by seeking to see more of the glory of Christ in the Scriptures (2 Corinthians 3:18).

Hope Joyfully Sings

A Hope-filled life ought to be a joy-filled life and, thus, a life filled with songs of praise. God calls his people together on a regular basis, and one of the very special things believers do is praise him in joyful song. Romans 15:5–6 speak of the unity of a body of believers who together "with one voice glorify the God and Father of our Lord Jesus Christ." Ephesians 5:18–19 speak of Spirit-filled Christians "addressing one another in psalms and hymns and spiritual songs, singing and making melody to the Lord." We sing corporately and also individually. This is because God has put a new song in our mouths (Psalm 40:3). The psalmist speaks of praising God "more and more" (Psalm 71:14). This is surely because as time goes on, we recognize more and more how great the salvation we have been given is (Psalm 71:15–16). We sing songs of thanksgiving to the God who saved us and loves us with an everlasting love (Psalm 146:3–5; 147:11).

Our joyful singing should always be with reverence and awe. "Therefore let us be grateful for receiving a kingdom that cannot be shaken, and thus let us offer to God acceptable worship, with reverence and awe, for our God is a consuming fire" (Hebrews 12:28–29). We must always conduct ourselves with the fear of the Lord. When God saves us, he doesn't change from being a holy God to something less. He doesn't ever change! He is holy and we must have an attitude of fear before him. Fearing God is not incompatible with hope and joy. Second Corinthians 7:1 speaks of our pursuit of holiness with the words, "bringing holiness to completion in the fear of God." He does not become a kind of permissive being who no longer cares about our behavior after we are saved. The grace that saves us is now working to transform us, and we must remember that God has written his law on our new hearts and given us his Spirit so that what the written code of the law could not do, will now be done, to at least some degree. We do not go about in our Christian life simply presuming upon God's favor. We do not say "He loves me so much, he lets me live as I want." We should say: "He loves me so much, he is changing me to be like him."

Now, we must be discerning about what this fear of God for the believer is and is not. It is not a fear of terror. We know our heavenly Father is perfectly good in all his ways. It is hard to think God wants us to live in the joy of the Lord while at the same time living a life being terrified of the Lord. However, it is clear that we must live in fear of the Lord. It is a fear of respect and reverence of the highest degree, a respect and reverence due only to God. We must recognize that our God is holy, and we must be in awe of his holiness. Our heavenly Father is worthy of the utmost respect, reverence, honor, praise, glory, worship, and love. We are not terrified, but we are humbled by his glory and grace. So, we should stand before him in reverence. We must sing praises to him with reverence and awe. Corporate worship isn't about entertainment and fun. It is about worship with thankful and joyful hearts that desire to praise our great God. The fear of the Lord must not be watered down so that it means little or nothing. Theologian Tom Schreiner says: "there is a kind of fear that does not contradict confidence."[1] Christians are to walk with confidence in Christ and joy in Christ. Hope and a healthy fear of God go together. Singing and reverence go together. Hope joyfully sings with reverence and awe.

The Hope That Sings Always Has Christ in View

Jesus Christ is the essence of our hope. Paul speaks of "Christ Jesus our hope" in 1 Timothy 1:1. Our singing must have Christ in view. I am not saying that every Christian hymn must mention Jesus, but I am saying that we always sing with the hope of redemption filling our hearts. Christ's cross and resurrection are the very foundation of our hope. We must sing songs filled with sound doctrinal truths about the redemptive story that is central to the Scriptures. The Scriptures tell us that Christ is our very life. Please do not misunderstand. We worship our triune God who is Father, Son, and Spirit. We worship one God not three. The Father, Son, and Spirit are not three parts of God. God is one in essence. He exists in three persons but each person possesses the eternal fullness of God. Thus, when we worship the Son, the Father is indeed glorified as well. The Spirit who is prompting our worship is also glorified. So we sing away giving praise to our Redeemer.

We must sing as those who know our real identity. Colossians 3:3 says some significant things about who we are in just a few powerful words: "For you have died, and your life is hidden with Christ in God." Let's examine it closely. It occurs in the context of Paul's encouragement for believers to focus on Christ and his kingdom. Christ's kingdom has become the realm we live in and our hearts and minds ought to be set on his kingdom's purposes and values (Colossians 3:1–2). Then, in Colossians 3:3, Paul points to two profound truths.

1. Thomas R. Schreiner, *The New American Commentary, I,1 Peter, Jude, Vol37* (Tennessee: B&H Publishing Group, 2003), 81

First: "For you have died"

Paul frequently teaches us the redemptive reality that not only did Jesus die for me, but that, in my union with Christ, I died with him. The old self is gone. I have been taken out of the old realm of evil. Although Paul doesn't use the word *risen* here, it is clear that the next part of the verse speaks of our being risen with Christ in a particular way: "and your life (our new life) is hidden with Christ in God." So, I have indeed been raised with Christ. I await bodily resurrection. A glorified body is an important part of my eschatological hope (Romans 8:23). Nonetheless, right now, I am a new creation. If you are a believer, you have been raised with Christ. The old you is gone. You are not the same person you were. So, Paul now describes the new life you now have.

Second: "Your life is hidden with Christ in God"

What does this mean? By emphasizing different parts of this text (*in God, with Christ, is hidden*), we can bring out at least something of the richness of this expression of our new and real identity as those who have died and are risen with Christ. The text says that our lives are hidden with Christ *in God*. We are secure in God. Being in Christ means that we are in God. We are connected to God in a real way, in a secure way. Nothing can separate us from him. In him, we are sheltered from the day of trouble. It is not that we will not experience trouble, but nothing can separate us from his love in the midst of it. We are sheltered from the day of trouble in that we are sheltered from its ultimate evil. Now, we must notice that our lives are hidden *with Christ*. We are intimately close to Christ. The text uses the word *with* here and not the word *in*. Of course, we are truly in Christ. The idea however here is that the union we have is close. We are hidden *with* him. The union is personal. The preposition *with* is suited "to express intimate personal union with [Christ]."[2] We are so close that in the very next verse Paul uses the expression

---

2. Peter T. O'Brien, *Word Biblical Commentary, Colossians, Philemon* (Nashville: Thomas Nelson, 1982), 170

"Christ who is your life." Then we must also notice that our lives are *hidden* with Christ in God. We are in some ways concealed. One way we are concealed is in the reality that what we are to be fully has not yet appeared. When Jesus comes we will know the fullness of our new self (1 John 3:2). Another way we are concealed is that although we can have close fellowship with other believers, there is something about us that the world cannot understand and just doesn't get. The new me with Christ in God is real. Thus: I am safe; I have hope; I am close to Christ; I am no longer estranged from God; Christ's life is flowing through me. Nonetheless, I know there is something more that is infinitely greater than I can understand! We sing as those who know something about who we are in Christ and who also know that our best life is not actually now, but when Christ appears. This is why we sing right now. This is why Christ is at the heart of our singing. A hope-filled life is a life of worship and praise and thanksgiving to our wonderful God. We will actually sing forever with everlasting joy (Isaiah 51:11; Psalm 89:1).

9

Hope and Glorification

In what is known as the *ordo salutis* (Latin for "order of salvation"), glorification is what happens last. The order is meant to be a logical sequence not strictly chronological, because some elements occur simultaneously in terms of time. However, glorification is last both logically and chronologically. In his classic work *Redemption Accomplished and Applied*, John Murray states, "Glorification is the final phase of the application of redemption. It is that which brings to completion the process which begins in effectual calling."[1] This is the *completion* Paul is pointing to when he tells the Philippian believers in Philippians 1:6, "And I am sure of this, that he who began a good work in you will bring it to completion at the day of Jesus Christ." So, we might say that our glorification is the final product of our redemption. Paul speaks of our eagerly awaiting glorification in Romans 8:23: ". . .we ourselves, who have the firstfruits of the Spirit, groan inwardly as we wait eagerly for adoption as sons, the redemption of our bodies." Paul goes on to speak of glorification as a central aspect of our hope in Romans 8:24–25: "For in this hope we were saved. Now hope that is seen is not hope. For who hopes for what he sees? But if we hope for what we do not see, we wait for it with patience." Paul sees hope as an intrical part of our

1. John Murray, *Redemption Accomplished and Applied* (Michigan: Wm. B. Eerdmans Publishing Co., 1955), 185

Christian life. He sees hope as a looking forward to the part of our salvation that is not yet realized. We hope for glorification when our redemption will be complete. I would like to briefly point out four truths related to our final glorification. These are things we must certainly set our hope upon.

Glorification Is When the Believer Will Receive a Glorious, Resurrected Body Like Jesus Christ's Resurrected Body

God's goal for his children is not incorporeal (without a body) eternal existence. Although to die is gain for the believers for at death the soul departs to be with Christ (Philippians 1:21–23), that is not our great hope. Our great hope is resurrection. The hope is to be like Christ. We are now God's children; what we will be has not yet appeared or been made fully known. Here is how John puts it in 1 John 3:2: "Beloved, we are God's children now, and what we will be has not yet appeared; but we know that when he appears we shall be like him, because we shall see him as he is." This means that we cannot fully comprehend not only what life will be like in the eternal state but what we will be like in the eternal state. However, we do know this: we shall be like Jesus because we shall see him as he is. The image of God we were originally created in will be restored completely. Upon seeing Christ at his appearing, there will be a transformation of whatever separates us from a full likeness at that time. Again, this is not referring to a believer's dying and being with Christ in what theologians call the intermediate state. This is referring to his coming again and the resurrection of the saints. This is what we are even now waiting for. "But our citizenship is in heaven, and from it we await a Savior, the Lord Jesus Christ, who will transform our lowly body to be like his glorious body, by the power that enables him even to subject all things to himself" (Philippians 3:20–21). John is speaking in 1 John 3:2 of a particular seeing of Christ and being given a body like his glorified body. This is how we will be in Christ's kingdom in the presence of God, worshipping and enjoying him and his abundant blessings forever. Please understand, we will not become gods, just human beings in the fullest way possible in accordance with God's ultimate design and with the goal of glorifying God forever and ever! John goes on to speak of how this hope that we have right now, motivates us right now. "And everyone who thus hopes in him purifies himself as he is pure" (1 John 3:3). John is saying that those who have this hope, purify themselves as Christ is pure. We desire to pursue holiness. We desire to make progress spiritually.

Believers Will Indeed Be Glorious, but Our Glory Will Simply Reflect the Glory of Jesus Christ

Jesus speaks of the righteous in God's eternal kingdom shining like the sun (Matthew 13:43). There is no doubt that we can describe glorification as glorious. In 1 Peter 5:1, Peter speaks of being "a partaker in the glory that is going to be revealed." Paul speaks of the purpose of our calling to be that we "may obtain the glory of our Lord Jesus Christ" (2 Thessalonians 2:14). It is proper for us to understand that whatever glory we will have is simply a reflection of the true glory of Christ. Our glory is not cause for self-exaltation. It is certainly true that we will appear with him in glory when he appears (Colossians 3:4). It is our great privilege to reflect the glory of Christ! The ultimate privilege is further that we behold his glory. This was part of Jesus prayer for us in John 17:24: "Father, I desire that they also, whom you have given me, may be with me where I am, to see my glory that you have given me because you loved me before the foundation of the world." The result of our glorified state is that God would ultimately be glorified. Oh, how we should anticipate with joy the day we are as sinless as Christ is sinless. How much we should long for the day when are hearts are as filled with delight in the Father as we reflect the glory of the Son.

Our Joy Goes Beyond What We Will Become and Ultimately Rests on the Fact That We Will Joyfully Be in God's Presence Exalting Him; God Is Ultimately All in All

As we see that our glory reflects Christ's glory, and we see that there is no room in our eschatological hope for self-glory, where does that leave us in terms of joy? In our self-oriented culture, it is needful that we see that both our joy now and our joy in the future is a joy in God not self. It is not that we do not delight in God's gifts and graces. It is not that we do not delight in the fact that God loves us. It is not that we do not delight in what we will become after this present evil age ends. We delight in these things and much more. Yet, we understand that what we will become is for the purpose of glorifying and enjoying God. Our delight in God's gifts point us to the giver. He is God and in his presence is the fullness of joy. We must not think of our hope as some kind of future exaltation of self. We are so pleased that we are God's chosen, set-apart ones, and beloved (Colossians 3:12). And we also recognize gladly that this is to the "praise of his glorious grace" (Ephesians 1:6). All things redound to God's glory (Romans 11:36).

In 1 Corinthians 15:24–28, Paul is unfolding some truths involved in the final destruction of what Paul calls "the last enemy" which is death. The great climax of this section is when all things are subjected to Christ and then Christ hands over the kingdom to his Father so that "God may be all in all" (v.28). Just as the offering of the firstfruits of the crops represented the consecration of the whole harvest to God, the kingdom of the resurrected saints, those in Christ, are now fully consecrated to God and they are handed to the Father. In this act, Jesus is saying: "here, Father, I want you to be glorified in all of this!" In an act of voluntary subordination pertaining to his human nature, the Son delivers the kingdom over to his Father so that God will be all in all. This means that the Father, Son, and Spirit can be enjoyed and glorified forever among the saints. Jesus' delegated or mediatorial kingly rule is now turned into the rule of God dwelling with his people. God, who is Father, Son, and Holy Spirit, will reign in Trinitarian glory forever. That is our ultimate joy.

Glorification Is the Finish Line of the Race Set before Us; It Is This Race We Must Run with Endurance

Hope drives us toward the finish line. Hebrews 12:1 speaks of the "race set before us." The idea is that we are still running. The race doesn't end at conversion. It just begins. We will go through many trials and afflictions. We must endure hardness. We must press toward the finish line. Hebrews 12:1 encourage us to run with endurance. The goal is to, as Paul put it, fight the good fight, finish the course, and keep the faith (2 Timothy 4:7). God is making us holy. We must strive for this holiness apart from which no one will see God (Hebrews 12:14). Believers can strive with the confidence that God will get us there. Sinclair Ferguson puts it this way: "God is a single-minded God. He is absolutely determined to make me holy. What makes me think that I can be indifferent to—or worse refuse and resist—his good purpose?"[2] We have assurance that we will persevere for we are kept in the faith by God's power, and his very Word continually promises our security. However, the Christian life isn't an abstraction. We live it. We must live it in light of glorification. Should we die before Christ comes, we rejoice in the truth that our souls go to be with Christ. I believe that even in this "intermediate state" we long for the fullness of God's kingdom to come.

I have never been much of a runner. Long distance runs especially were never my specialty. I admire those who can endure for long distances. I am amazed at their stamina and determination to finish the race. Many run these long-distance marathons not to win but simply to finish. That alone is a great accomplishment. But the race set before us as believers is different. There is a joy set before us that is worth it all. I believe that we could also say that there is a hope set before us, thereby calling this particular joy part of our eschatological hope. The truth is that saying as is sometimes said, "It will be worth it all," is a huge understatement. The finish of this race is actually just the beginning! I can think of no better way to close this chapter than with Paul's words in 2 Corinthians 4:16–18: "So we do not lose heart. Though our outer nature is wasting away, our

2. Sinclair B. Ferguson, *Devoted to God: Blueprints for Sanctification* (Edinburgh: The Banner of Truth Trust, 2016), 209

inner nature is being renewed day by day. For this slight momentary affliction is preparing for us an eternal weight of glory beyond all comparison, as we look not to the things that are seen but to the things that are unseen. For the things that are seen are transient, but the things that are unseen are eternal."

10

The Deception of Appearances

As a pastor for some 38 years, I have seen numerous people go through many situations that appeared hopeless. These are truly days lived out in a fallen and finite world. By *hopeless* here, I mean a situation where something seems radically wrong. This could not possibly be happening. God seems very much out of the picture. It can be hard for believers to recognize that God is always working as promised. Even when things do not seem to make sense in our eyes, we must understand that God always knows exactly what he is doing. Nothing takes him by surprise. He is in sovereign control of every molecule of the universe. On Mount Carmel, the prophet Elijah mocked the false god named Baal. Baal's prophets were trying to cry out for Baal to bring down fire from above to consume their sacrificial offering. Nothing was happening. I love how 1 Kings 18:29 puts it: "but there was no voice. No one answered; no one paid attention." Elijah mocked by wondering out loud among other things if Baal was on a journey or asleep. After the false prophets failed, Elijah prepared an altar and sacrifice and prayed to the living and true God who immediately answered with fire (see 1 Kings 18:20–40 for the whole account). Our God does not sleep. He does not take vacations. "Our God is in the heavens; he does all that he pleases" (Psalm 115:3). Our God is always in full control of everything. From his perspective, there are no accidents—no mistakes. In this chapter, I would like us to consider three very interesting accounts in the redemptive narrative where it might have seemed that something had gone wrong. The point being in each case that we must always rest in God for he can be fully trusted!

A Sickness Seemingly Gone Wrong

In John 11:1–44, Lazarus, of Bethany died. Lazarus had two sisters, Martha and Mary. John 11:5 says, "Now Jesus loved Martha and her sister and Lazarus." It is clear that Jesus had a special relationship with this family. In the beginning of the chapter, we find that Jesus is told about Lazarus' illness and Jesus states that "this illness does not lead to death. It is for the glory of God, so that the Son of God may be glorified through it" (John 11:4). Jesus says that he will act for the glory of God. Yet, at the same time, John 11:5–6 tells us that Jesus loved this family such that "when he heard that Lazarus was ill, he stayed two days longer in the place where he was"! The text seems to be indicating that out of love Jesus waits until Lazarus dies before going to him. How is it loving to let Lazarus die? When Jesus does get to Bethany, Martha certainly wishes that he came sooner (v.21)! As it turns out, this was not a sickness gone wrong, but an opportunity for the glory of God to be displayed in Lazarus' being raised from this death.

Appearances (Christ's waiting two days before going to Bethany) would seem to say that Jesus does not really care about Lazarus, Martha, and Mary. But then we see Jesus weeping (v.35) and desiring to display God's glory to Martha, Mary, his disciples, and the people around them (v.40). Out of this event comes one of the great truths of the Scriptures as Jesus tells Martha, "I am the resurrection and the life. Whoever believes in me, though he die, yet shall he live, and everyone who lives and believes in me shall never die." (John 11:25–26). Appearances can be deceiving. We must embrace the truth that ultimately God's glory is the absolute imperative while, at the same time, he works all things together for the ultimate good of his children. We may not understand at the moment. In fact, we may not understand all the while that we remain in this present evil age. We must trust God at all times, even when it doesn't seem to make sense to us. We must let hope sustain us through times when things seem hopeless. For the believer, there is no more hopelessness.

Sons Seemingly Taken Away Forever

Now, let's go back somewhat further in redemptive history, all the way back to Genesis. The patriarch Jacob had 12 sons. Ten of the sons sold their brother Joseph to a band of Midianite traders who brought him to Egypt and sold him to an Egyptian named Potiphar, an officer of Pharaoh. Joseph went through a series of trials but eventually God brought him to a prominent position in Egypt, second only to the Pharaoh. God had revealed to Joseph through Pharaoh's dreams that there would be seven years of plenty in Egypt followed by seven years of famine. Under Joseph's direction, this allowed Egypt to be prepared for the famine and to actually sell food to surrounding nations during the famine. Thus, Joseph's ten brothers (the very ones that sold him) find themselves before Joseph in Egypt to get food though they do not know it is him. After inquiring about their family, Joseph demands that one brother of the ten be kept in Egypt and that the other nine brothers go back to their father and bring back to him their younger brother, Benjamin. So Simeon stays in Egypt and the other brothers go back and tell their father Jacob that this Egyptian leader has demanded that Benjamin be brought to Egypt. Jacob responds with great distress. Listen to his words: "You have bereaved me of my children: Joseph is no more, and Simeon is no more, and now you would take Benjamin. All this has come against me" (Genesis 42:36). Here are some great misstatements, all because of the way things appear. "Joseph is no more." Actually, Joseph is alive and well and God is using him to save your family, Jacob. "Simeon is no more." No, Simeon is alive and well and being taken care of in Egypt. "Now you would take Benjamin." But not to harm him. And here is the climax of these misstatements: "all this has come against me." In reality, God is using all these things for good, Jacob. He will save your family from this famine. They will multiply in Egypt. God will deliver them from bondage. God will bring them into the land of promise. Through them, God will bring forth the Messiah. Through them all the nations of the earth will be blessed. Now, we must acknowledge that it certainly seemed like things were against Jacob. The lesson once again is that God must be trusted at all times. "Trust in him at all times, O people; pour out your heart before him; God is a refuge for us" (Psalm 62:8).

God's Kingdom Seemingly Defeated by Satan, Roman Authorities, and Jewish Leaders

Here is what must have been for Christ's early followers the most confusing time of their lives. Jesus has been crucified! Listen to the two disciples on the Emmaus Road as they spoke of Jesus of Nazareth: "But we had hoped that he was the one to redeem Israel" (Luke 24:21). They were bewildered because Jesus has been crucified. Of course, the irony here is glorious, for they are speaking this to the resurrected Christ who just did redeem God's true Israel. The cross, which appears to be Christ's defeat is actually where Jesus defeats sin, Satan, and death. It is where Jesus saves sinners. God forbid that we should glory in anything else (Galatians 6:14). To help us see the crucifixion from a proper perspective, let's ask and answer some simple questions with the Word of God.

Does Pilate or anyone else really have authority to take Jesus' life? Pilate arrogantly said to Jesus when Jesus was silent in Pilate's presence: "You will not speak to me? Do you not know that I have authority to release you and authority to crucify you?" (Luke 19:10). Christ replied: "You would have no authority over me at all unless it had been given you from above" (Luke 19:11). Pilate's so-called authority was only given him to accomplish God's ordained purposes. The truth is that Jesus is laying down his life for his sheep. No one is taking it from him. Jesus makes this clear in John 10:17–18: "For this reason the Father loves me, because I lay down my life that I may take it up again. No one takes it from me, but I lay it down of my own accord. I have authority to lay it down, and I have authority to take it up again. This charge I have received from my Father." So, we see, the Roman authorities can only do what they do because Christ is laying down his life voluntarily! The appearance of Christ failing to bring in God's kingdom was deceptive. He did not fail. his death was a necessarily part of the plan. He gave his life to be a ransom for many.

Here is another similar question we could ask. Was God's redemptive plan foiled by Christ's enemies in the crucifixion of Jesus? Did the Jewish leaders, certainly the enemies of Christ, thwart what Jesus was trying to accomplish? In actuality, they were doing exactly what God foreordained. Peter put it this way in Acts 2:23 in his sermon on the day of Pentecost: "This Jesus, delivered up according to the definite plan and foreknowledge of God, you crucified and killed by the hands of lawless men." Notice that Peter is charging at least some in his Jewish audience with crucifying and killing Jesus Christ. However, we must also notice that that their delivering Jesus up to the Romans for crucifixion happened according to the definite plan and foreordination of God. God's purposes were not thwarted but fulfilled by them, while, at the same time, they were guilty of this great sin. God's foreordination does not excuse them; they are accountable. Yet, in the end, God's ordained purposes are simply being unfolded in history. We must not forfeit here the accountability of human actions because of God's sovereign will being accomplished. Scriptures teach us that both are true. My point here is that no one foils God's redemptive plans. There is another great passage of Scripture that shows us both the wickedness of those who crucified Jesus and God's sovereign purposes being worked out in the very same act of crucifixion. "For truly in this city there were gathered together against your holy servant Jesus, whom you anointed, both Herod and Pontius Pilate, along with the Gentiles and the peoples of Israel, to do whatever your hand and your plan had predestined to take place" (Acts 4:27–28). No! God's redemptive plan was not frustrated; it was fulfilled!

One last question is in order. Is hope lost as the two disciples on the Emmaus Road seem to be wondering in their statement in Luke 24:21: "But we had hoped that he was the one to redeem Israel." Again, the answer is absolutely not. All is truly well, and hope, real hope, lives on. In fact, he (Jesus, our hope) literally lives on! Appearances may look quite bleak, when, in fact, all is going according to plan. Are you a believer? Then, you are not hopeless, because your hope is not wishful thinking but rests firmly in that which God has promised his children through Jesus Christ. Can things appear to be going wrong? Yes, they can. Can we sometimes be tempted to despair? Yes, we can. But God calls us to trust in him, and he can be fully trusted. How the truth of Romans 8:31 needs to be embraced: "If God is for us, who can be against us?" It is a rhetorical question which categorically is to be answered, "no one can be against us in the ultimate sense of thwarting God's good purposes for us."

11

Hope and Suffering

This chapter could also be titled "A Hope That Does Not Disappoint." It is based on Romans 5:3–5, verses that teach us a great deal about how God cultivates hope in his children. One of the ways God does this is through suffering. Paul, in Romans 5:1–2, has stated that, since all believers have been justified by faith (been counted as righteous in Christ), they have peace with God. Not only peace with God, but access to the grace in which they stand. Believers also are those who rejoice in hope of the glory of God. These are such wonderful gospel graces! Yet, Paul goes on to make a truly remarkable statement that we must surely listen to. In Romans 5:3, Paul writes, "More than that, we rejoice in our sufferings." Paul is not saying that believers are stoic in their sufferings or complain their way through them or be angry at God through them. He says that we rejoice in them! Sufferings in this verse (the Greek word *thlipsis* which literally means *pressure* or *pressing together*) refers to the sufferings or troubles that result from life's circumstances—the pressures, the afflictions, the pains, the agonies—all the bad things that life in a fallen world can throw at us. It refers to all the different kinds of suffering in this life. It is a strong word. It is not talking about some mere inconvenience, but it speaks of things that come our way that we might consider troubles or evils or trials. I once heard someone describe our trials as anything that would cause us to say "oh no! Not this!" How can this be that a believer in Jesus Christ would rejoice in his or her sufferings? Why would anyone do such a thing? Well, Paul goes on to explain. We must keep in mind that this does not mean that the sufferings in and of themselves are good. They are, indeed, sufferings, and they came into the world as a result of sin. They will be eliminated some day when the fullness of God's kingdom is brought in. So, we don't call the sufferings themselves good. Yet, in the midst of them, we are to rejoice. Beyond that, because of them, we rejoice. Paul is not simply calling for a joy in God while one suffers. Paul is pointing to a joy in God because of the suffering. This is not simply a rejoicing during our sufferings, but a joy because of them. Yet, it is not because we are strange people who enjoy pain, but because God is using these sufferings for good. Paul gives us some compelling reasons to rejoice in sufferings. I want to point out five statements implied in Romans 5:3–5 that explain our rejoicing in our sufferings.

These Truths about Suffering Are Meant to be Known

Paul starts to explain why we would rejoice in sufferings with the words "knowing that." He is appealing to the fact that Christians should know and need to know some things, and understanding that God has an important reason for suffering is one of the things we must know. What Paul wants us to know here is this: suffering produces hope. The text gives us a kind of logical chain involving what suffering produces. We may well ask: "How does suffering produce hope?" Particularly when part of our eschatological hope is that in the eternal kingdom of God there will be no more suffering! So the chain goes like this: "knowing that suffering produces endurance, and endurance produces character, and character produces hope" (Romans 5:3b-4). It is important also to understand that in the long term, this ultimately succeeds because God is the one doing the work—working all things together for our ultimate good (Romans 8:28). This is a grace-driven sequence, and God's grace is decisively at work in all of these aspects. God's salvic purposes for his children do not fail.

Suffering Moves the Genuine Believer toward God Not Away

So, we see first of all that suffering produces endurance. This means that suffering produces in us a steadfastness of faith. We keep on keeping on. We keep running with endurance the race set before us (Hebrews 12:1). The Romans passage we are referring to uses the word *produces* three times. It means that God is bringing about something. Suffering, for the believer is producing endurance of faith. Now, one would think that suffering would cause just the opposite. It would cause one to quit the faith. So we must see the role God's enabling grace plays here. In our suffering God ultimately moves us to look to him. It causes more and more humble reliance upon our loving heavenly Father. We will look more closely at this in the next chapter when we discuss how God even brings hope out of despair. The heart with no faith can move away. Suffering can make the unbeliever as Martin Luther says: "more carnal, weak, blind, wicked, and irritable."[1] Yet, by God's grace, he moves our hearts toward him in suffering. He is our refuge and fortress as Psalm 46:1 clearly tells us: "God is our refuge and strength, a very present help in trouble."

Endurance, Over Time, Changes Us to God-Reliant People

The next part of this spiritual sequence is this: endurance produces character. Our endurances, over time, change us into those who are God-reliant. They change our character or who we are on the inside. In our sufferings, our hearts are being changed by God! As we, over and over, experience the sufficiency of God's grace to uphold us, strengthen us, and bear us up under the afflictions, our *spiritual* character (which is certainly in view in this text) is grown. Understand that the sequence here is not simply steps. These are things that happen over time. Our responses are not always consistent. Yet, God is faithfully doing his work in our hearts and he enables us to make some progress.

1. Martin Luther, Commentary on Romans (Michigan, Kregel Classics, 1976), 90

Character is translated "proven character" in the New American Standard translation and I think this gives the best sense. It is a quality that comes through tests of time. As a Christian endures a particular episode of suffering and relies on God, their faith is a little more proven and they have become a more God-reliant individual. We become, over time, more veterans of the faith, so to speak. Rather than rookies, we have learned and grown. However, no believer ever fully arrives in this lifetime. In fact, none of us ever come close. We are to be always humbly learning and growing, taking small steps in our pilgrim journey of faith. This is not to say that we never temporarily fail a test of faith. It is to say that we never completely fall away, because this is all a work of God's grace. Over time, we are more and more, individuals who look to Jesus, the "author and finisher of our faith" (Hebrews 12:2 KJV).

Indeed, grace comes to us truly because Jesus now prays for us as our great high priest, and the Father answers his prayer. Consider what Jesus told Peter as recorded in Luke 22:31–32, "Simon, Simon, behold, Satan demanded to have you, that he might sift you like wheat, but I have prayed for you that your faith may not fail. And when you have turned again, strengthen your brothers." Right after this, Peter temporarily failed by denying that he knew Jesus. Peter later repented and turned again to the Lord, such that after Christ's resurrection, the Lord said to Peter essentially three times: "feed my sheep" (John 21:15–17). Jesus office of priesthood continues. We can take great comfort in the words of Hebrews 7:23–25, "The former priests were many in number, because they were prevented by death from continuing in office, but he holds his priesthood permanently, because he continues forever. Consequently, he is able to save to the uttermost those who draw near to God through him, since he always lives to make intercession for them."

We must certainly not think of character here in secular terms but in spiritual terms. God is making us into humble people who understand their own weaknesses and rely on Christ's sufficient grace (2 Corinthians 12:7–10). Christian character is not about becoming a proud, self-reliant, self-made man or woman. It is about walking in a humble, dependent, and submissive posture before God, and he uses suffering as one means to accomplish this.

God-Reliance Is at the Center of a Believer's Hope

Now the next part of this spiritual sequence is that character produces hope. This is because God-reliance is at the very center of a believer's hope. Hope is our reliance upon (confident assurance in) God's promises to be fulfilled because we believe God to be faithful. So we rejoice in suffering not simply because we can say like many other people (even unbelievers): "I believe that there is some kind of purpose to everything." The problem with the way people say this many times is that it is so vague.

Paul here wants us to know this: the God of the Bible—the God who has saved our souls has specific purposes for our sufferings and one of them is to produce hope. God's faithfulness in our sufferings helps us understand that faithfulness is at the essence of his being. He is faithful to finish what he began. He has promised this to us. In Philippians 1:6, Paul conveys this confidence in God's faithfulness to the believers in Philippi: "And I am sure of this, that he who began a good work in you will bring it to completion at the day of Jesus Christ." God is faithful. We see it in so many verses. Paul is saying that we are also meant to experience it as our Christian life unfolds. Our suffering becomes a schoolhouse for experiencing God's grace not merely as an abstract concept but as a reality in our lives. This is not to say that in a particular episode of suffering, there will always be deliverance or relief. This is to say that, for the believer, there will always be grace! It will be grace that moves us to God. It will be grace that allows us to know his presence through the trial (Hebrews 13:5). It will be grace that allows us to experience his strength.

Hope Does Not Disappoint Because
God's Love Cannot Disappoint

If I boast among my friends that my favorite team is going to win the big game in spite of the fact that they are serious underdogs, and they lose big, then I am disappointed (or put to shame) by my presumptuous boasting. If I get myself all worked up and excited about going out with some friends to some new restaurant, but the meal I have is not so good, then I am disappointed. But Paul closes out this passage by stating that suffering ultimately produces a hope that will not put us to shame or as some translations have it "does not disappoint." The sense in the text is future. The eschatological (future) hope we have in Christ will in no way disappoint! We will not have to hang our heads in defeat on the day of reckoning. We will not have to be ashamed. This is, of course, all of Christ's doing. He is the victor. He is worthy of all the praise and glory. No one who trusts in the living and true God will ever be disappointed that he or she did so. It should be clear to us that God's promises cannot disappoint. In 2 Peter 1:4, Peter speaks of believers having been granted "precious and very great promises." I like the King James Translation which refers to the promises of God as "exceeding great and precious"! Yet, we must go further in Romans 5:5 and look at the words "because God's love has been poured into our hearts through the Holy Spirit." The love in this verse is referring not to the giving to us of love for God or others (which is true, of course), but it is pointing to the Spirit's pouring into our hearts of the love God has for us. We know God's love for us because the Spirit has made us new creations in Christ. This is not God pouring into my heart my worthiness for I am unworthy. This is not God pouring into my heart a knowledge of how wonderful I naturally am, because I am naturally a sinful person. God pours into my heart that he loves me with an everlasting love to the praise of his glorious grace. Thus, our hope is made that much more wonderful and certain. It comes to us by way of God's everlasting, unfailing love. God's great love speaks to us about the fact that he has rescued us from the wrath to come and brought us into a relationship of everlasting blessedness with him. This is the love that nothing can separate us from (Romans 8:37–39). This is the love that Paul prays for the Ephesian saints to comprehend the breadth and length and height and depth of—the love that surpasses knowledge (Ephesians 3:18,19). This is the love that allows us to have confidence for the day of judgment and casts out a terrifying fear of God (1 John 4:17, 18).

How can it be that one could rejoice in one's sufferings? We can rejoice because ultimately our sufferings bring about a real, genuine, unfathomably glorious hope. We have a hope that will never disappoint. Suffering is the path to glory God has chosen for us, and one of the ways God matures us in the faith. Suffering matured Job, Joseph, Moses, David, and Paul. We too must be humble learners in God's schoolhouse of suffering. It leads us to more and more reliance upon Christ and his sufficient grace. Perhaps you already understand that suffering is a part of life in a fallen world. However, you must go further in your understanding. Suffering has a significant purpose in the life of a Christian. A Christian's suffering is working *for* him or her. It is producing endurance, character, and hope. May we rejoice in the midst of our sufferings because we know that God is at work in our hearts!

12

Hope Out of Despair

In Chapter Six, we examined some of the enemies of hope. In this chapter, we want to look at one particular enemy of hope close up. The enemy is *despair*. In the last chapter, we looked at suffering. This chapter is closely related, and I will say some of the same things. However, despair warrants some further examination and we will look at a key passage concerning it. Despair many times arises from suffering. It is certainly a suffering of the soul. Let me define how we are using this word: Despair is the great anxiety and extreme fear, often accompanied by an utter lack of ability to bear up, that can be present when one is under enormously difficult circumstances. I have heard it said about a few people that they never get down and out. I find that hard to believe. Despair is a real malady of a broken-in-sin world. I do not think we should be so naïve as to think our enemy would not seek to drive us to this state of mind. So, we want to examine how God himself brings his children hope in the midst of immensely difficult circumstances. Paul's words in 2 Corinthians 1:3–11 bring out some very significant thoughts on this matter, so I will be referring to this text throughout the chapter.

God Is, of Course, the Key in Lifting
a Believer out of Despair

Let us begin by looking at the very strong language Paul uses to indicate the extreme state of his afflictions in 2 Corinthians 1:8: "For we do not want you to be ignorant, brothers, of the affliction we experienced in Asia. For we were so utterly burdened beyond our strength that we despaired of life itself." Whatever the specific circumstances Paul was going through, it is clear that they were beyond his own ability to bear up under them. This is despair. I cringe when I hear believers utter the words, "I know that God will never give me anything that I can't handle." It expresses, whether intentionally or not, an unhealthy self-reliance. Instead, we ought at all times to seek a spiritually healthy utter dependency upon God. God brings our way what he determines will ultimately move us to look to him. He does not give us anything that he cannot handle. He may well give us things way beyond our own strength. Paul expresses such a burden beyond his own strength. He was brought to a place of despair of life itself. Now, let's look back at how Paul begins this chapter by describing God. "Blessed be the God and Father of our Lord Jesus Christ, the Father of mercies and God of all comfort, who comforts us in all our affliction, so that we may be able to comfort those who are in any affliction, with the comfort with which we ourselves are comforted by God" (vv.3–4). God is the God of all comfort! God is the God who comforts his children in all of their affliction. It is God that lifts the despairing soul out of the darkness of affliction. He does this not necessarily by removing all of the problems but by actively working in the heart bringing assurance of his presence and his strength. We must know that Christ promises his presence at all times. He will never forsake us (Hebrews 13:5). This does not simply mean that he is there, but that he is actively present working for our ultimate good continually. Listen to the Psalmist's expression of hope during affliction: "Remember your word to your servant, in which you have made me hope. This is my comfort in my affliction, that your promise gives me life" (Psalm 119:49–50). God comforts us in affliction. He is the God who lifts his children out of despair.

God Does Not Promise an Affliction-Free Life

Paul states in 2 Corinthians 1:4 that God comforts his children in all of their affliction. We must notice then the assumption that there will be affliction in the Christian life. We discussed suffering in the last chapter and how God, through suffering produces hope. It is certainly true that everyone living in the present world can expect some troubles, for this world is fallen and inhabited by fallen and finite creatures. Ultimately the death sentence is upon all human beings. As Eliphaz said in Job 5:7, "Man is born to trouble as the sparks fly upward"! Believers are not exempt from all that this fallen world might bring to people in terms of natural disasters and diseases. You may have noticed that Christians have car accidents and Christians get cancer. Christians have people-problems and Christians even have church-related problems. Christians also to some degree or another will suffer persecution for the faith (2 Timothy 3:12). As I mentioned in Chapter 11, I remember someone describing a trial as anything that caused one to say, "Oh no, not this!" Well, I confess, I have said that (or at least thought it) more than a few times in my life. Sometimes we say, "Oh no, not this; not now!" In this chapter, I am especially referring to afflictions of an extreme nature. I believe that we will all have at least a few of those if we live long enough. Yet, it is also true that God will give some of his children more than others. Not all of us will die the death of a martyr. Not all of us will experience the constant pain of some excruciating long-term illness. But it is important for us to know that the life of a believer is not supposed to be easy. I cannot stress enough that the path to our eternal glory in Christ is a path of suffering (1 Peter 4:1). As Jesus said, "In the world you will have tribulation" (John 16:33).

God Uses our Affliction Experiences to Comfort Others Going Through Similar Experiences

Though there may be many reasons for our afflictions (such as the building of hope), we must understand that one of them is that we might be able to comfort other believers who go through the very same things. Let's look at 2 Corinthians 1:4 again: "who comforts us in all our affliction, so that we may be able to comfort those who are in any affliction, with the comfort with which we ourselves are comforted by God." So here is one of the ways God may comfort a believer—through another believer who has experienced something similar. I believe the verse also means that we can be comforted by another believer in our afflictions who has not experienced a similar affliction but has experienced the great comfort of God and can attest to God's faithfulness. The important point is that those who know the comfort of God pass this on to others who need the comfort of God. He is the God of all comfort and sometimes he uses the means of comforted saints to bring his comfort to the afflicted.

When my wife and I were very young in the Lord, having both been saved a few months apart when we were both twenty-seven years old, we lost a child. It was an extremely difficult situation. Shortly before her due date, we found out that the baby's development was not normal. Ultrasounds were somewhat new back in that day, but the ultrasound showed an enlarged head. The baby was delivered by Caesarean section and rushed to the special neonatal nursery. Shortly after that, we received word that he had passed. Upon delivery, they showed us our baby and let us touch him. He had severe facial deformities. We had only been Christians for a few months. I think the only verses we knew were Proverbs 3:5–6, "Trust in the LORD with all your heart, and do not lean on your own understanding. In all your ways acknowledge him, and he will make straight your paths." God used these verses to give us comfort. When I look back on that time, I know that it was God who sustained our faith, gave us the comfort we needed, and grew us through his Word. Sure enough, over the years, we have been able to comfort others who have experienced similar afflictions. When we lost our son, I never dreamed for a moment that I would some time later officiate at the funerals of others who lost children in similar ways. I was certainly able to tell them of God's faithfulness to comfort his children as he had comforted me. Mary was able to speak words of encouragement and grace to grieving parents just as God had comforted her heart during our particular affliction. I certainly do not know all of the reasons God took our son to be with him after just a few moments of life, but I do know that we knew his mercy and comfort and peace. I also know that he has used that experience to allow us to minister to others who have experienced similar afflictions.

Though There May Be Many Reasons for Our Affliction, We Must Realize That a Main Reason Is So That We Abandon Hope in Anything or Anyone Else but Him

Now we come to the heart of the 2 Corinthian text: "Indeed, we felt that we had received the sentence of death. But that was to make us rely not on ourselves but on God who raises the dead" (v.9). Paul states that he felt like his affliction was a sentence of death. Then, he immediately follows by expressing his understanding that, God wasn't using this affliction to kill him but to make him more dependent. We spoke in the last chapter of God using suffering to grow us in God-reliance. Severe suffering has the ability to shout this out to our hearts. God is showing us that we must humbly accept that he is in control and that he has ultimate good for us in mind. One of the most important questions that you can ask at any time in your Christian life is this: "Who am I depending upon?" God wants us to recognize our absolute need to depend upon him at all times. Another way of saying this is that these severe afflictions are intended to bring us to our knees before God as his children. They help us recognize that unless he gives us strength we will not have any strength of significance. Besides this, God wants us to recognize that he is glorified in our humble dependency. That is how he designed our salvation in the first place. He chooses what is foolish to shame the wise. He chooses what is weak in the world to shame the strong (1 Corinthians 1:27). He saves through Christ so that our boasting is in him alone. Our salvation is in him alone. Our boasting is in him alone. Our hope is in him alone. Paul realizes that this severe affliction, this despairing episode, was to move him into more reliance upon God. Notice that Paul states that our reliance is on "God who raises the dead." This reminds me of 1 Peter 1:3 which tells us that we have "a living hope through the resurrection of Jesus Christ from the dead." Our ultimate deliverance is not from physical death. Our affliction may well be an illness that leads to our physical death. Our reliance goes beyond the grave to resurrection. This is what Jesus means when he tells Martha in John 11:25, "Whoever believes in me, though he die, yet shall he live." How we must see that our hope is all wrapped up in Jesus Christ, and that, in him, it is secure!

Prayer Is a Major Instrument God Uses for our Deliverance

One final point that Paul makes in all of this is the means of prayer God uses to deliver his saints from despair. In 2 Corinthians 1:11 Paul continues to relate his despairing event: "You also must help us by prayer, so that many will give thanks on our behalf for the blessing granted us through the prayers of many." He says that these Corinthian believers can help him by prayer. He says that one result of their prayers could be that many will gives thanks on behalf of Paul's deliverance. The prayer of many can result in the thankfulness of many. When we are in the midst of a time of severe affliction, we should not hesitate to ask for prayer. This is one of the blessings God graciously provides for us in the local church. We are certainly to pray for one another. In a local body, we must bear one another's burdens. At the same time, we must also be willing to bear our own load. (Galatians 6:2–4). I believe that one of the principles in this passage in Galatians is that there are some burdens that we must deal with. There are normal duties and hardships in life that we are to carry personally. We must not burden others with every stress of our lives. However, there are some afflictions, trials, and despairing circumstances that must be shared with others. The primary way we can do this is by a simple prayer request.

Prayer request times at a local church through small groups or otherwise can be very interesting. There are some believers that do not seem to see life's different circumstances as being on various levels of distress. In other words, everything seems to be a major crisis. "Pray for me, I have a tire that has a slow leak" seems to be on the same level as "I just lost my job." I would prescribe, all things being equal, that the slow leak would not require corporate prayer, but certainly, in most cases, a job loss would. I rarely ask for prayer for normal health issues. I was, however, very eager to ask for prayer when my wife was going to have coronary by-pass surgery. We must bear some burdens and share others. I am sometimes amazed when believers will make health issue requests for loved ones and friends but never make salvation requests for these same people though it seems clear that they are not believers. May God grant us wisdom in the area of prayer requests. Nonetheless, in those truly potentially despair-causing events certainly God uses the prayers of the saints for deliverance. Great is our joy and thanksgiving when God answers prayer.

In 2 Corinthians 1:3–11, Paul reveals his personal despair and points to God as his only hope. He even expresses confidence that God will continue deliver him. Notice v.10: "He delivered us from such a deadly peril, and he will deliver us. On him we have set our hope that he will deliver us again." God will keep on delivering his children one way or another until he takes us home. We must recognize that he has his appointed time for even our final breath. So, we must set our hope upon him. In times of despair, look to the very anchor of your soul, Jesus Christ (Hebrews 6:18–19).

13

Gracious, Gospel-Centered Hope

God graciously gives believers genuine hope through the gospel of Jesus Christ. Hope is gracious because we do not merit it. We are underserving. Hope is gospel-centered because Christ did earn it for us. There is a real sense in which he purchased our hope on the cross. He purchased our hope. He is our hope. We live because he lives, and he lives because he defeated death on the cross. His resurrection is the affirmation that death has been defeated. His resurrection is the new humanity brought forth because of his triumph over Satan, sin, and death—the triumph that took place on the cross. We participate in this resurrection because his death made atonement for our sins. We continue to look to him because there is salvation in no other. In this chapter, I would like to examine three of the most gospel-centered hope passages in all of Scripture. As we look at them, I believe our response should first of all be, "How great is our God!" This response should be followed by, "How great is our hope!"

Passage One: Christ, the Center of Gospel Hope

The mystery hidden for ages and generations but now revealed to his saints. To them God chose to make known

> how great among the Gentiles are the riches of the glory
> of this mystery, which is Christ in you, the hope of glory.
> (Colossians 1:26–27)

Paul's letter to the Colossians magnifies the glorious person and work of Christ. In the passage we want to examine, Paul is discussing his personal ministry of preaching the gospel. In Colossians 1:25, Paul explains that he has been given a stewardship or a commission from God to make the word of God fully known. These verses (vv.26–27) explain what Paul means by making the word of God known in its fullness. Paul is saying that his commission is about making the mystery fully known. Just what does Paul mean by *mystery*? Here is a working definition of how this word *mystery* is used in Scripture: *mystery* refers to the revelation of things partially hidden in the past that have now been revealed more fully through gospel light.[1] Some things are hidden to us and known only to God. Some things are revealed in Scripture, many times progressively. Some things were only seen in shadows in the Old Testament. The New Testament brings these things into clearer light. Paul's task was to proclaim and explain the mystery (that which had been somewhat hidden for ages and generations but had now been revealed) pertaining to the gospel of Jesus Christ (v.26). In fact, *mystery* can refer to the entire gospel as in Romans 16:25: "Now to him who is able to strengthen you according to my gospel and the preaching of Jesus Christ, according to the revelation of the mystery that was kept secret for long ages." Sometimes *mystery* can refer to one particular aspect of the gospel. In 1 Corinthians 15:51, the mystery is that not all believers will experience death but that all believers will be resurrected, as Paul refers to Christ's second coming: "Behold! I tell you a mystery. We shall not all sleep, but we shall all be changed."

Many things were revealed to the apostles who then revealed them to the New Testament saints. So, Paul explains in v.27 that God chose the New Covenant saints to be the recipients of this mystery. The emphasis here is that the revelation of this mystery was to all the saints including the Gentiles. God desires all of his people to

---

1. For an excellent exploration of the New Testament concept of *mystery*, see Beale and Gladd, *Hidden But Now Revealed.*

know the riches of the glory of this mystery. The revelation of these things specifically to the Gentiles is a part of this mystery. In other words, it has been made clear that the Gentiles would be included among God's people. But at the end of v.27 Paul describes this mystery by referring to the heart of it: "Christ in you, the hope of glory." The shadows and types of the Old Testament pointed to something or more accurately someone, but it was not clearly discernable. But now it is clear. What was shadow, is now substance. Christ's person and work have become clear. Redemption by the Son of God is no longer partially hidden but has been accomplished and is being explained by God's apostles. Christ has not only come but is now, in fact, dwelling in every believer through the Spirit of God! One of the central features of God's covenantal purposes was that God would dwell with his people and be their God—that, in fact, is how redemption's story will end (Revelation 21:3). In the Old Testament we have the tabernacle and then the Temple where God met with Israel. Those shadows have now been replaced with Christ himself dwelling in his people through his Spirit. Someday we will be in the presence of Christ in his glory. We look for the blessed hope of his coming recognizing that he is gloriously on the throne at the right hand of his Father. However, it has been revealed to us that he is also *in* us. We know from other New Testament Scripture that we are indwelt by the Spirit of Christ. The Holy Spirit does not come to replace Christ, but to bring Christ to us! Right now, it is Christ in us "the hope of glory." This should be understood with the sense of "hope for glory." A good paraphrase for this would be: "Christ in you giving you assurance of experiencing the presence of his glory." Here is how Paul expresses it in Titus 2:13, "Waiting for our blessed hope, the appearing of the glory of our great God and Savior Jesus Christ." While we are awaiting the appearance of his glory, our hope is not only in heaven but also in us! Our hope is real. The Sprit of God brings Christ to our hearts even as he shows us more and more of Christ's glory through the Word of God.

As with many biblical mysteries, thought we define them as revelation that was once partially hidden but now revealed, they contain truths that have an element of incomprehensibility to them. I cannot fully explain *Christ in me*. However, I know that my union with Christ is a real one. It is not simply a picture of my relationship with him, but a real organic union—I am in him and he is in me. He has changed me, is still changing me, and will someday complete what he began. His glorious redemptive work on the cross has brought the hope of eternal life to my very soul!

Passage Two: Christ, Our Sure and Steadfast Anchor

> So that by two unchangeable things, in which it is impossible for God to lie, we who have fled for refuge might have strong encouragement to hold fast to the hope set before us. We have this as a sure and steadfast anchor of the soul, a hope that enters into the inner place behind the curtain. (Hebrews 6:18-19)

In the context, the above verses are part of an admonishment for believers to have the full assurance of hope to the very end. Believers are to be those who through faith and patience inherit the promises. The writer of Hebrews then explains the certainty of God's promises. His promises are guaranteed by (as our text tells us) "two unchangeable things." Those two things were presented in Hebrews 6:13-17. They are God's word and his oath. God cannot lie. His word is truth. Then, for the sake of our human weaknesses, God affirmed his word with an oath. However, God could not swear on anything higher than himself, so he swore by himself! The point is simple. His promises are guaranteed. All of this was done to give us "strong encouragement to hold fast to the hope set before us." God has laid out the great eschatological promises before us. There is Christ's coming for us and the resurrection of the body (and it will be a glorious body like Christ's). There is the renewed heavens and earth, a kingdom with no more sorrow or suffering, no more sin, and no more curse. There is God himself dwelling with us. There is enjoying God forever and ever. These are guaranteed and they provide us with strong encouragement to endure until they are enacted.

The writer goes on to say that this hope is our soul's sure and steadfast anchor. The language here represents the fact that our hope is completely stabilizing. Notice, however, that our hope enters into the inner place behind the curtain. This is picking up the language of the Tabernacle and then the Temple in the Old Testament. The high priest would enter behind the curtain with a blood sacrifice once a year on the Day of Atonement on behalf of the people of Israel. A little later in Hebrews, the author will explain that the Old Testament offering was a foreshadowing of Jesus' offering. He entered the presence of God on the basis of his shed blood to secure our eternal redemption. He is our hope. Hebrews 6:20 goes on to explain that Christ is our forerunner. He entered first into the presence of God as our high priest to provide us access to God. Please think about this next truth: our hope is so secure that even now through Christ, we have access to the Father! In fact, Paul sees this access to the Father as cause for our rejoicing in hope: "Through him we have also obtained access by faith into this grace in which we stand, and we rejoice in hope of the glory of God" (Romans 5:2). So not only has Christ brought this glorious hope to my soul through my union with him, but also brought hope to my soul by giving me a hope that can now enter the throne room of God through Christ.

Passage Three: Christ, Our Living Hope

> Blessed be the God and Father of our Lord Jesus Christ! According to his great mercy, he has caused us to be born again to a living hope through the resurrection of Jesus Christ from the dead, to an inheritance that is imperishable, undefiled, and unfading, kept in heaven for you, who by God's power are being guarded through faith for a salvation ready to be revealed in the last time. (1 Peter 1:3–5)

Peter, in the opening words of his first letter, has referred to believers not only as God's chosen ones but also as exiles. He is saying that if you are a Christian then you are a kind of stranger to this world's cultures. You are an exile or pilgrim—a resident alien. We believers live here in this world, but it is not our permanent home. Our values are different. We think differently. In fact, we exist in a whole new realm than the unbelievers who are currently this world's natives, so to speak. So right at the beginning of his letter, Peter begins with the truth that Christians, those who are truly strangers in this world, have a living hope that sustains them. I may be a pilgrim, but I have stability, security, and staying power for as long as I am here. We have a life of hope that only God's people can have. Christian pilgrims are the only human beings that have true hope. All others are hopeless unless they too come to Christ. By the way, the world as a body of people is not our enemy but our mission field. Our hope should be visible and shared. We will visit that thought in our final chapter. For now, however, we want to consider two great truths that Peter points out concerning our hope in Christ.

First, Peter affirms the great truth that the believer's hope is established by God. God wants you to have hope and to have it abundantly. He wants your hope to be sustaining and satisfying. Our hope moves us to worship. That is why we find Peter in verse three exclaiming "Blessed be the God and Father of our Lord Jesus Christ!" When we bless God it simply means that we speak well of him or make much of him. To bless God means to speak about God with a heart overwhelmed with his goodness and grace toward us redemptively. It should not be hard for those once hopeless to praise God for the living hope we have in Christ. Because God establishes our hope, we find it full of vitality. He has caused us to be born again. We are new creations in Christ. This is purely by grace. We do not contribute to our spiritual birth any more than we contributed to our physical birth. It is God's work and it is a real work, not simply a good feeling. God has changed our hearts. Hope has life and not deadness. It is full not empty. Peter also points out that God establishes our hope in Christ. He is the source. Notice Peter specifically refers to Christ's resurrection from the dead as being a source of this hope. Our hope is living because Christ has been raised from the dead and is alive evermore. It has been secured by historical events. The gospel includes Christ's death on the cross for our sin and his resurrection on the third day. We live because Jesus lives. He is the firstborn of many. God establishes our hope.

The second truth we want to focus on is this: our hope includes an inheritance that is reserved in heaven for us. The word *kept* in the text can also be translated *reserved*. Notice that this inheritance is imperishable (not subject to death or decay), undefiled (it can never be spoiled by sin), and unfading (it will never lose its beauty; it is free from the ravages of time). This hope is secured by God. Verse 5 teaches us that God preserves us in the faith. Salvation will be fully revealed at the end of the age and we will be waiting for it. Our reservation is secure. When the text says that our inheritance is reserved in heaven for us, it doesn't mean that our inheritance is heaven (for we are looking for the new heaven and earth ultimately), but that the reservation is kept by God who is in heaven. No one can destroy this reservation. Nothing can annul it. We not only know Christ is bodily in heaven and will return at the appointed time, but we also know that our inheritance is reserved with a certain security that only God can guarantee.

Three Glorious Perspectives on the Believer's Hope

The three passages above give us such wonderful perspectives on biblical hope. Yes, we look outside of ourselves to Christ who is our hope. However, because of our union with Christ, we have an intimate connection with our hope beyond our comprehension but nonetheless real to us. Yes, our hope is secured by God's word and his oath. However, because this sure and steadfast anchor of our souls has led the way as our forerunner into the presence of God by his blood, we too can come into the Father's presence with confidence further affirming the sureness of our hope. Yes, our hope is established by God. However, we know that our future inheritance in the kingdom has been reserved for us with complete security. It is a reservation made by God and protected by God. This is the gracious, gospel-centered hope that we have. How great is our God! How great is our hope!

14

Practical Wisdom for Enriching and Exercising Hope

This final chapter has a kind of "where the rubber meets the road" theme. That expression points to the fact that hope for the believer needs to be more than an abstraction. It needs to be in the everyday living out of our lives. A runner can prepare and train, but the race is where the "rubber meets the road." However, I am not going to present formulas or steps or techniques here to cultivate hope in your life. There is a lot more involved in living the Christian life than just a few steps to follow. We must not reduce the Christian life to a "sanctification-by-decision" thing. This happens when some teaching is given and one simply "makes a decision" to follow it. Unless those decisions are undergirded by a sound understanding of truth, brought about as one looks to Christ and not oneself, and brought forth by God's grace, they will ultimately come to naught. Another path we want to avoid is the "sanctification-by-procedure" route. Spiritual life is just not designed that way. Christian living is not programmatic. God is transforming our hearts. We are all at different places in that progressive work of God. Salvation is about God saving sinners so that they might glorify and enjoy God forever. Although being transformed, believers can still to some degree (though not absolutely) be: stubborn (Hebrews

3:8,12),unrepentant (James 4:8–10), proud (Romans 12:3), selfish (Colossians 3:5), opinionated (1 Corinthians 8:1–2; Romans 14:10), self-reliant (Galatians 3:10), and more. The sanctification process requires a number of things going on simultaneously, such as: soul nourishment (Hebrews 13:9), continual repentance (James 4:8–10), growing faith in what union with Christ means (Romans 6:11), increasing trust in God that he will do what he has committed himself to do (Philippians 1:6; 2:13), serious and continual prayer (Colossians 4:2), and much more. There are no magic formulas or instantaneous maturity strategies. Yet, there is real growth through God's ordained means. So do not look at what follows as a formula or series of steps. Think of these things as biblical encouragements for building hope and exercising hope. They are not exhaustive but serve to offer some concrete and practical things to think about as you seek by God's grace to live a hope-filled life.

Keep Holding Fast to the Hope Set before You (Hebrews 6:18)

If you are a believer, God is holding you securely. Nonetheless, you need to hold firmly to Christ. Your holding comes by his decisive grace. But hold on—cling tightly—don't let go. The temporal pleasures of this world cannot in any way compare to knowing God and most especially to being known by God (Galatians 4:9). How can one turn back to anything else when one has experienced God's amazing grace and glorious being? Christ is your anchor, your refuge, your strength, your life, your all. You are secure in him, but remember that, at the very same time, we through faith and patience inherit the promises (Hebrews 6:12). We are to have proper assurance not arrogant presumption.

Seek to Have Word-Shaped Reflection (Psalm 119:11) and Word-Shaped Prayers (Luke 1:38)

Spend time meditating on God's word. Reflect on the great truths. Reflect on God himself, his wondrous being, his great works.

Grow in your understanding of truth. Grow in your knowledge of Christ. See more and more of his glory in the unfolding story of redemption in Scripture. Reflect Biblically. Recognize that God has ordained growth through the means of the preaching and teaching in the local church through properly appointed servants with the gifts to do these tasks. Seek to develop listening skills. Receive with meekness the implanted word, which God uses in the ongoing sanctification process (James 1:21). Go over and over texts of Scripture. Hide them in your heart. Meditate on the many verses on hope (many which are found in this book).

Then pray God's word back to him. Be like Mary in Luke 1:38 who after receiving the angelic message, said, "let it be to me according to your word." If God says, "May the God of hope fill you with all joy and peace in believing, so that by the power of the Holy Spirit you may abound in hope" (which he does say in Romans 15:13), then pray, "God please fill me with joy and peace; help me believe more and more. May I be filled with hope by the power of your Spirit." Let what you meditate upon become the substance of your prayers as suits particular texts.

Talk to Yourself About Hope in Christ (Psalm 42:5,11; 43:5)

The psalmist asks himself why his soul is cast down and in such turmoil. Then the psalmist answers with hope! "Hope in God; for I shall again praise him, my salvation" (Psalm 42:5,11; 43:5). Don't answer with the ways of the world but with the word of God. Continually focus on all of the grace of God found in the gospel. Our hearts are strengthened by grace (Hebrews 13:9). The gospel is good news. You cannot save yourself. You cannot sanctify yourself. Do not slip away into self-dependency. Humbly rely upon God. We seem wired to think in terms of meriting by self-performance before God. Our blessings as believers, every one of them, have been secured by Christ. He is our hope. Continually remind yourself of this truth from the various texts that proclaim it.

Don't Move Away from the Gospel but Grow Deeper in It (Colossians 1:23)

I was brought up in a Christian culture that falsely taught that the goal of the church was to win people, wet them (baptize them), and work them. Once one was saved, it was time to be busy serving God. We came to the cross for salvation, then we were off and running on our own. That is not the way it works. We must recognize that God doesn't actually need us. He is quite capable of running his world and building his church (Acts 17:24–25). We could not serve apart from his gifting us (or giving us breathe for that matter). I am not saying that God does not use us. We should desire to be a vessel for honorable use, but we must recognize that we serve God's people by his grace and for his glory. But all the while, we must be growing ourselves. We must nourish our souls. We must grow deeper in gospel truths that strengthen our hearts! Paul encourages the Colossian church not to shift from the hope of the gospel (Colossians 1:23).

Never Think of Money or Material Possessions as an Object of Hope (1 Timothy 6:17)

In 1 Timothy 6:17, Paul warns us not to put any hope in the uncertainty of riches. Our hope is always in God. We must not make material objects our gods. We must not make money our god. The temptation is great to treasure wealth. Paul earlier in chapter six of 1 Timothy warns against the very desire to be rich (v.9). God may bless us with good things, and it is not wrong to enjoy them. In fact, it is right to enjoy them and be thankful for them. What we must be sure to do is look beyond our good gifts to the giver and be sure we are loving and worshipping him and not the temporal things. Also, we must use our possessions and finances for God's glory and kingdom purposes. There is no intrinsic hope to be found in money. It cannot bring us peace or joy or satisfaction. True peace, joy, and satisfaction are to be found in God alone.

Understand That Your Hope Will Not Be Understood by Unbelievers for It Goes Against Their Perceived Realities (Romans 4:18)

In Romans 4:18, we are told that Abraham in hope believed against hope. This is in reference to the promise of an offspring in spite of the fact that Sarah and he were very old. What does it mean to hope against hope? I think it means that one's true hope in God's faithfulness seems against the odds, so to speak. One's hope seems to go beyond the reality of a situation (even though our hope is based on the reality of Christ's redemptive work on the cross and God's faithfulness). As Christians, we can expect many to look at our hope and think it is a pipedream. We are awaiting the return of Jesus Christ, the resurrection of the dead, the transformation of our mortal bodies into a glorious immortal body like Christ's, and a perfect kingdom of righteousness, peace, and joy. Don't expect everyone to jump up and down for joy concerning our hopes. In this world we face, skepticism, unbelief, scorn, and the like. But be of good cheer, for these things (righteousness, peace, and joy) have already been purchased by Christ and we will inherit the kingdom with him!

Understand Also That Hope Should Be Visible and Shared with Unbelievers (1 Peter 3:15)

On the other hand, everyone may not be scornful. Remember hope rejoices. Your joy might just catch someone's attention as God moves in one's heart. When it does, 1 Peter 3:15 tells us to be ready to give them an answer for our hope. Peter uses the word *defense* in this verse, meaning that our reasons should be soundly biblical and that we should make them clear. A hope-filled life should be visibly different. We are not only to be sojourners and exiles in this world, but we are also to be much different from the *natives*. We ought not to be the complaining, discontent, angry kind of people no one wants to get near. It should be evident that rather than being the most miserable of all people, our hope makes us the most joyful human beings (1 Corinthians 15:19). In humility, we ought to "look not only to [our] own interests, but also to the interests of others" (Philippians 2:4).

Focus on the Major Eschatological Events (1 Peter 1:13)

There is a significant amount of differences among believers regarding some details of future events. These differences occur between very theologically-sound Christians. It is wise for us to study these things and come to our judgments about them carefully. It is also wise to allow for acceptable differences that are within the scope of orthodoxy. This book is certainly not the place for a discussion of these matters. I am simply calling for graciousness among us over these non-essential issues. As many have said, some of these things are not unimportant, but they are not essential to the gospel. Among all the different views however, there are certain things that are most certainly believed. These are the very things foundational to our hope. They include: the literal, visible second coming of Christ (and that believers are to look for his coming), the resurrection of the saved and unsaved, the judgment of the unsaved to eternal hell, the glorification of the saved with resurrection bodies like Christ's, and the entrance of the saints into the new heaven and earth where they will worship and enjoy God forever. All of the major eschatological perspectives hold to these things. In 1 Peter 1:13, we are told to set our hope fully on the grace that is to come when Christ comes. There are so many glorious truths to set our hope upon. My warning here is simply this: do not be involved in the rampart speculation that goes on about the "end times." Do not read the Bible into the headlines and speculate about things uncertain. Understand that any speculation predicting the time of Christ's coming again is wrong (Matthew 25:13). We should always keep watch for we simply do not know.

The God of Hope Is Glorious

There is so much more that could be said about this hope that we have. In 1 Timothy 1:1, Paul uses these words: "Christ Jesus our hope." We wait for the day that we can worship before the throne confessing Jesus Christ as Lord to the glory of God the Father, because of the work of God the Spirit in our hearts. And now, "May the God of hope fill you with all joy and peace in believing, so that by the power of the Holy Spirit you may abound in hope" (Romans 15:13)!

Bibliography

Aitken, Jonathan. *John Newton: From Disgrace to Amazing Grace*. Wheaton: Crossway, 2007.

Beale, G. K., and Benjamin L. Gladd. *Hidden But Now Revealed*. Downers Grove: InterVarsity, 2014.

Caneday, Ardel B., and Thomas R. Schreiner. *The Race Set Before Us*. Downers Grove: InterVarsity, 2001.

Carus, William. *Memoirs of the Life of the Rev. Charles Simeon*. London: Hatchard, 1847.

Ferguson, Sinclair B. *Devoted to God: Blueprints for Sanctification*. Edinburgh: Banner of Truth Trust, 2016.

Gibson, David. *Living Life Backwards: How Ecclesiastes Teaches Us to Live in Light of the End*. Illinois: Crossway, 2017.

Luther, Martin. *Commentary on Galatians*. Grand Rapids: Kregel, 1979.

———. *Commentary on Romans*. Grand Rapids: Kregel, 1976.

Moule, Handley. *Charles Simeon*. London: Forgotten Books, 2012.

Murray, John. *Redemption Accomplished and Applied*. Grand Rapids: Eerdmans, 1955

O'Brien, Peter T. *Word Biblical Commentary, Colossians, Philemon*. Nashville: Nelson, 1982.

Packer, J. I. *Knowing God*. Downers Grove: InterVarsity, 1973.

Piper, John. *The Roots of Endurance*. Wheaton: Crossway, 2002.

Schreiner, Thomas R. *The New American Commentary*. Vol. 37, *1 Peter, Jude*. Tennessee: B&H, 2003.

———. *Run to Win the Prize*. Wheaton: Crossway, 2010.

Tripp, Paul David. *New Morning Mercies: A Daily Gospel Devotional*. Wheaton: Crossway, 2014.

www.ingramcontent.com/pod-product-compliance
Lightning Source LLC
Chambersburg PA
CBHW071051090426
42737CB00013B/2321